USBORNE FACTS OF LIFE



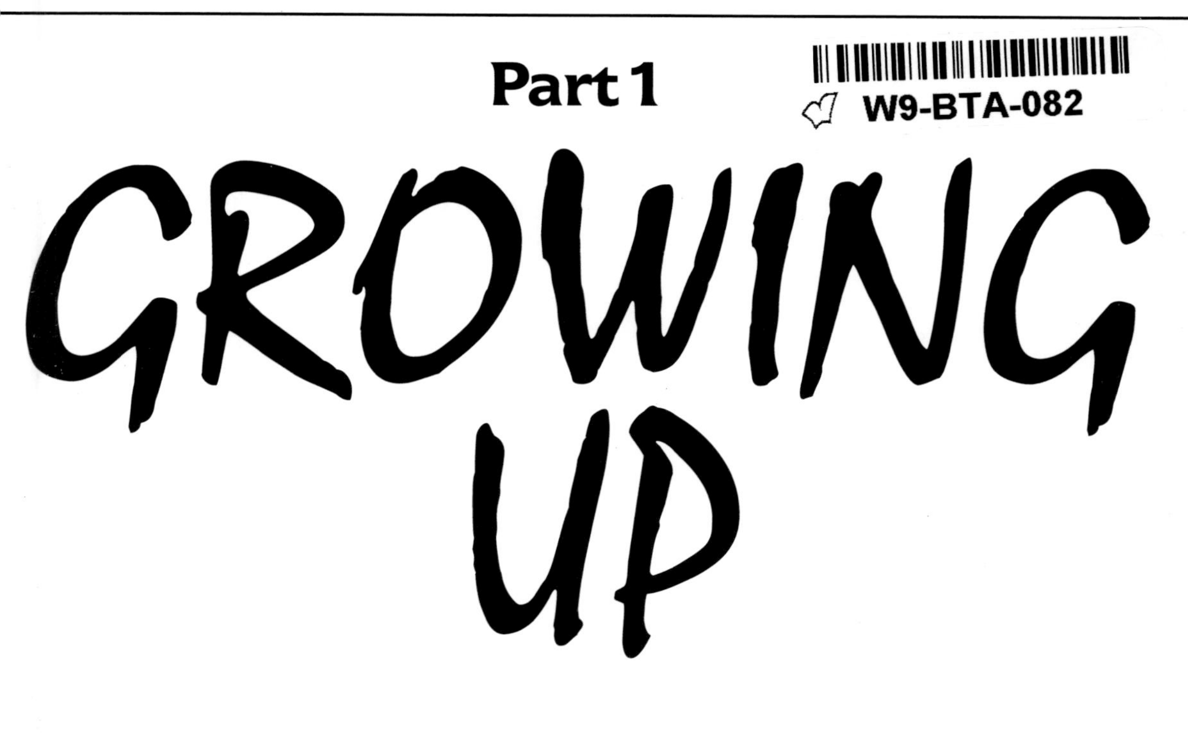


**Susan Meredith**

**Designed by Roger Priddy**
**Design revision by Isaac Quaye**

**Illustrated by Sue Stitt,**
**Kuo Kang Chen and Rob McCaig**

**Consultants: Judy Cunnington, Relate Marriage Guidance Council and**
**Fran Reader, Senior Registrar, Obstetrics and Gynaecology,**
**University College Hospital, London.**

# Contents - part 1




First published in 1985 by Usborne Publishing Ltd, Usborne House, 83-85 Saffron Hill, London EC1N 8RT, England.



First published in America in 1986. This edition published in America in March 1998. AE.
Printed in Spain.

# About part 1

You have been growing up since the day you were born. Just as a baby grows and changes as it becomes a child, so there is another, equally important, period of growth as you stop being a child and become an adult. This period is called adolescence, from the Latin word *adolescere*, which means to grow up.

## Adolescence

Adolescence lasts for several years, from the age of around 11 or younger up to the age of around 18 or older. It involves all kinds of changes, both to your mind and emotions (psychological changes) and to your body (physical changes). This book concentrates mainly on explaining the physical changes of adolescence.

## Growing

On the first few pages you will find out about growth at adolescence and what changes you can expect in your body shape and voice.

## Puberty

The physical changes of adolescence are called puberty, from the Latin word *pubertas* which means adulthood. Most of them take place in the early years of adolescence.

Pages 8-9 will give you a general idea of the changes of puberty, how they happen and when. Then, on the following pages, they are all explained in more detail.

## Sex and babies

The most important change of all is that you start being able to produce children so, on pages 16-33, there are sections on reproduction, sex and how contraception is used to prevent unwanted pregnancies.

## Your emotions

Although this book deals mainly with the physical changes of adolescence, your emotions are very important too. Some of the confusing feelings you may experience are discussed on page 43.

## Finding out more

You will find further information about things that affect your body, such as food and drugs, on pages 34-42. Then, on page 44, there is information about AIDS.

On pages 45-47 there is a glossary of difficult and technical terms. It includes definitions of some words that do not appear in this book but which you may come across elsewhere. On page 48 there are addresses and telephone numbers which may be helpful.

# Growing

One of the earliest changes of puberty is that you suddenly grow taller very fast. This "growth spurt" is triggered by substances called hormones, which are produced by special glands in your body. You will find out more about hormones and glands later on in the book.

During your growth spurt, you grow as fast as you did when you were two years old. When a boy is growing at his fastest, he usually adds 7-12cm (2¾-4¾in) to his height in a single year. Girls add 6-11cm (2¼-4¼in).

On this page you can find out about how you grow and when you are likely to stop.

## Height

**At age 10 ...**

The pictures above show the average height of males and females at different ages and the percentage of their adult height that has been reached.

Girls start their growth spurt at about 10½ and boys at about 12½ so, for a while, girls tend to be taller than boys. Boys catch up by the time they are 14, though, and they still have some growing to do while girls have almost finished.

## How tall will you be?

You can use the information in the chart on the right to estimate your eventual height. It tells you the percentage of your final height you are likely to have reached at any age during puberty. Here is the calculation you must do:

$$\frac{\text{Present height (cm or in)}}{\text{\% of full height (see chart)}} \times \frac{100}{1}$$

Here is an example for a boy, aged nine, who is 130cm tall:

$$\frac{130}{75} \times \frac{100}{1} = \frac{520}{3} = 173.3$$

This boy is likely to be 173.3cm tall when he has finished growing.

| Age | % Boys | % Girls |
|---|---|---|
| 8 | 72% | 77.5% |
| 9 | 75% | 80.7% |
| 10 | 78% | 84.4% |
| 11 | 81.1% | 88.4% |
| 12 | 84.2% | 92.9% |
| 13 | 87.3% | 96.5% |
| 14 | 91.5% | 98.3% |
| 15 | 96.1% | 99.1% |
| 16 | 98.3% | 99.6% |
| 17 | 99.3% | 100% |
| 18 | 99.8% | 100% |
| 19 | 100% | 100% |

Remember, all the ages and figures given in this book are averages only. Growth in height, like every other change of puberty, varies with the individual. The age at which you start your growth spurt bears no relation to your final height. This is determined mainly by what you have inherited from your parents. A few people do not go through a real growth spurt at all but just keep on getting taller very gradually instead.

## How bones grow

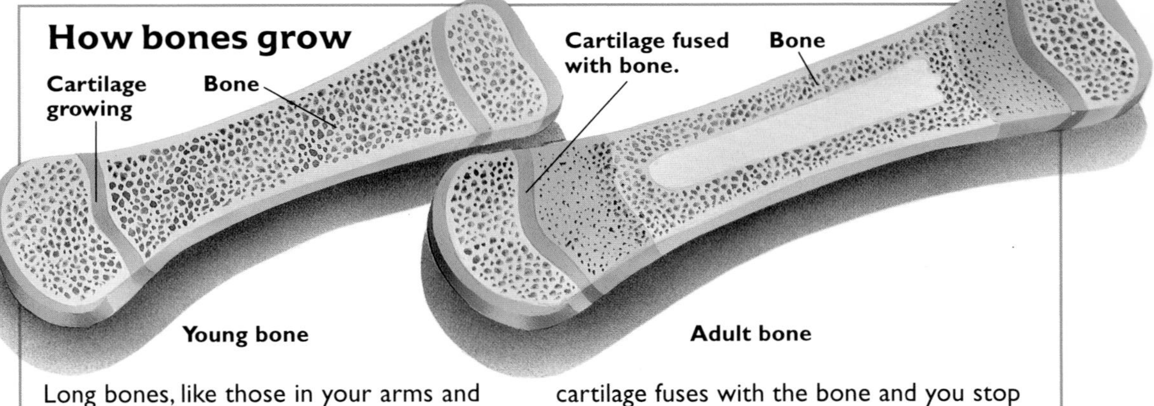


Long bones, like those in your arms and legs, contain a rubbery substance called cartilage near the ends. The bones grow longer as the cartilage grows. Eventually, under the influence of sex hormones, the cartilage fuses with the bone and you stop growing. One of the reasons women are generally smaller than men is that they become sexually mature earlier and so have less time to continue growing.

## Body shapes

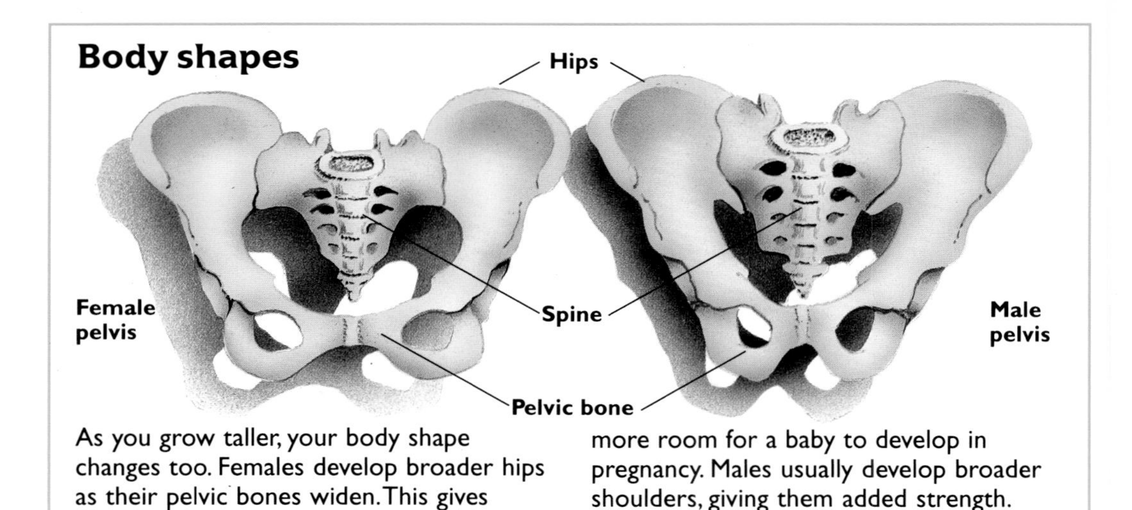


As you grow taller, your body shape changes too. Females develop broader hips as their pelvic bones widen. This gives more room for a baby to develop in pregnancy. Males usually develop broader shoulders, giving them added strength.

## Voice changes

As the rest of your body grows, your voice box (larynx) also gets bigger and this makes your voice deeper. Most people's voices change very gradually, but a few alter all at once. Males' voices go deeper than females' because males develop larger voice boxes. You can see this from the way the Adam's apple sticks out. Boys are sometimes embarrassed during puberty by their voices suddenly breaking into a squeak. This happens when the muscles of the larynx get out of control momentarily.

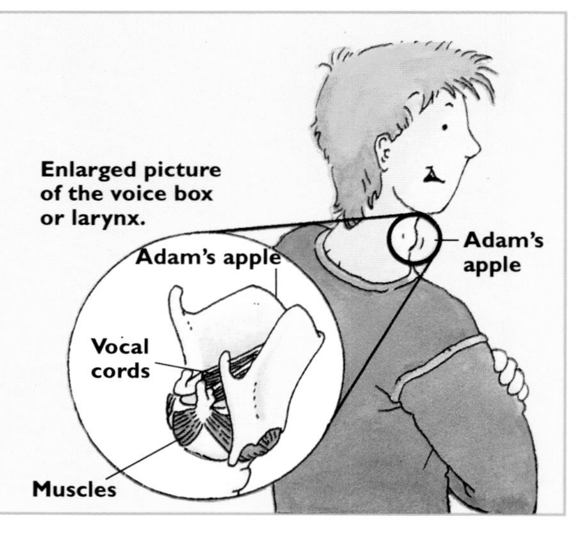


## Face changes

You will notice that your face alters quite a lot at puberty. Some people describe it as coming down from under the skull. Your nose and jaw both become more prominent and your hairline recedes. Boys' faces alter more than girls' do.

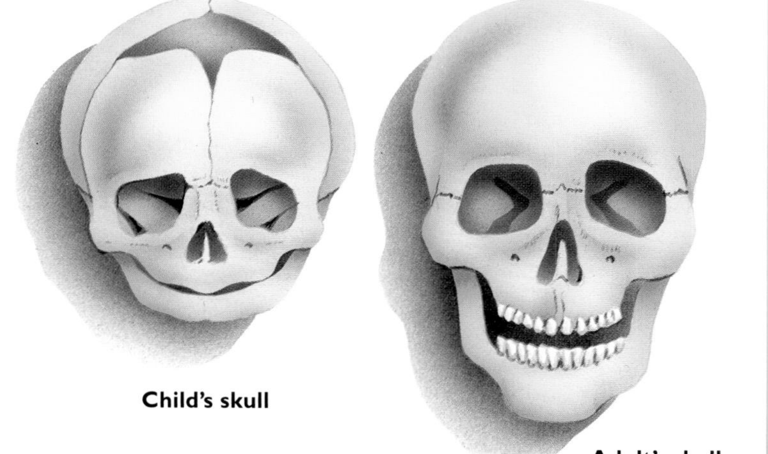

## Muscles

As you grow up, your muscles increase in size and you get stronger. At birth, around 20% of your body is muscle. This increases to around 25% in early puberty and around 40% when you are an adult. Men tend to have more muscle than women relative to their size. It is not true that you can "outgrow your strength" and so become weak and exhausted. Strength does lag behind size though, so you may look stronger than you really are for a while.

## Why are men stronger than women?

Usually, but not always, men are stronger and have more stamina than women. This is not only because of their size, shape and muscles but also because they develop larger hearts and lungs than women, relative to their size. The differences are often exaggerated by upbringing, if boys are encouraged to do more sports, for example, than girls. None of this makes men healthier than women and in fact women usually live longer.

## The "ideal" figure

Some people worry that they are not a certain shape or size. This is partly due to the "ideal" figures, especially of women, shown in advertisements, on TV, in films, in newspapers and magazines. In reality, different people find different body types attractive and, provided you are not very over or under weight, you do not need to worry.

## Feeling gangly

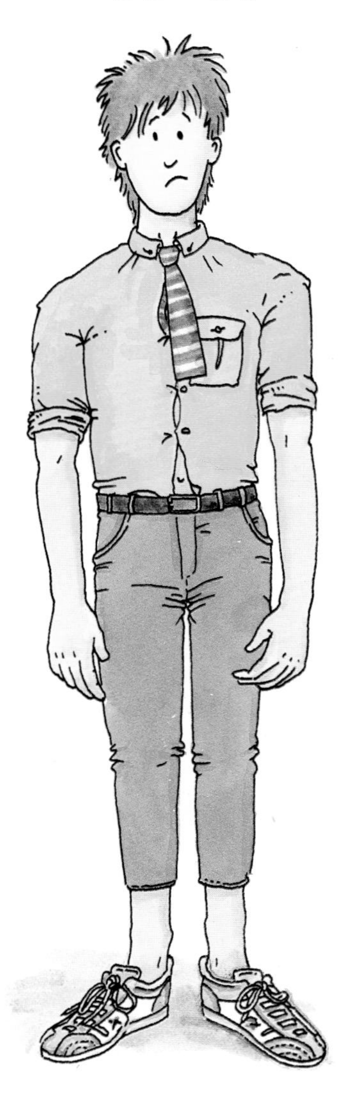

During your growth spurt, your body does not grow at the same rate all over. First, your feet and hands get bigger, then your arms and legs lengthen and, about a year later, the rest of your body grows. This may not be noticeable but some people are conscious of having oversized hands and feet for a while. It is not true that your coordination gets worse at puberty.

# What happens at puberty?

When you reach puberty, all sorts of different changes start taking place in your body. The main purpose of them all is to enable you to start producing children. The main change is that your sex organs* grow and develop, and start producing the special sex cells from which babies can be made. (A cell is the smallest individual living unit in the human body.) You are not really aware of some of the changes going on, because they take place right inside your body. Others are much more obvious. The pictures on the right show some of the main changes of puberty.

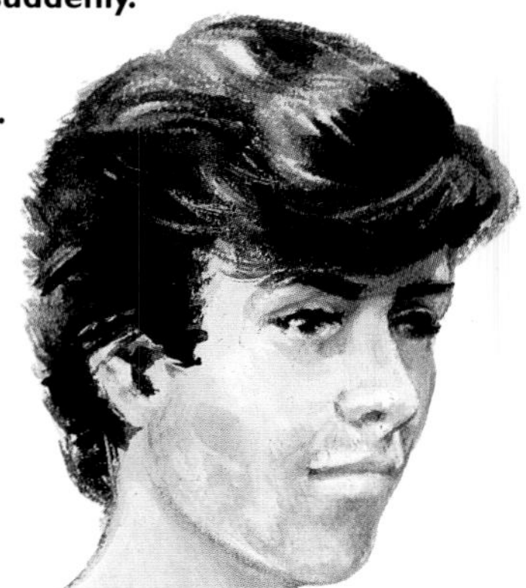


## Secondary sexual features

Some of the changes that happen at puberty, such as beard growth and breast development, are not essential for producing children. Unlike the sex organs, which are known as primary sexual features, these are known as secondary sexual features. They are attractive to the opposite sex, acting as a signal that you are different from them.

*An organ is any part of your body which has a particular job to do.*

Height increases suddenly.

Face alters.

Breasts develop.

Hair starts to grow under arms.

Hips widen.

The circle of bone formed by the hips is known as the pelvis. There is a picture of the pelvic bones on page 6.

Pubic hair starts to grow.

The ovaries, which are inside a female's abdomen, enlarge and develop. Female sex cells, called ova* or egg cells, develop in the ovaries. Periods start (see pages 20-23).

## When does puberty start?

The age at which people reach puberty varies between the sexes and also between individuals. The average age is usually said to be 11 for girls and 13 for boys. This is misleading, though, because girls can reach puberty any time between the ages of 8 and 17, and boys any time between 10 and 18.

This large timespan means that two people of the same age can be very different. One of them may have finished developing physically before the other has even started.

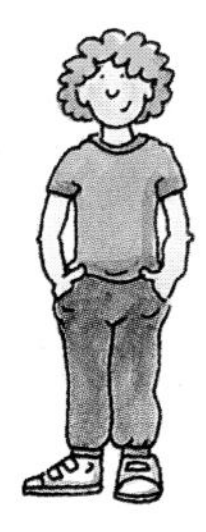

This sometimes causes embarrassment. It may help to realize that neither "early" nor "late" development is in any way abnormal. Nor is one "better" than the other.

The age at which you reach puberty doesn't affect what you will be like as an adult. Whether your body matures slowly or quickly, it will continue to do so until you are fully developed.

What determines the age you reach puberty is mainly the characteristics you have inherited from your parents. Your build may also play a part. Short, stocky people tend to develop earlier than tall, thin people.

*The singular of ova is ovum.*

# How puberty starts

The changes that take place in your body during puberty all start in your brain and are caused by chemical substances called hormones. During childhood, you have only low levels of certain hormones in your body and no one knows quite what they do. At puberty, your brain increases the levels of these hormones and this makes your body start producing the sex cells: ova or sperm. The level of other hormones, known as the sex hormones, also increases to bring about the rest of the changes of puberty.

## Your brain and puberty

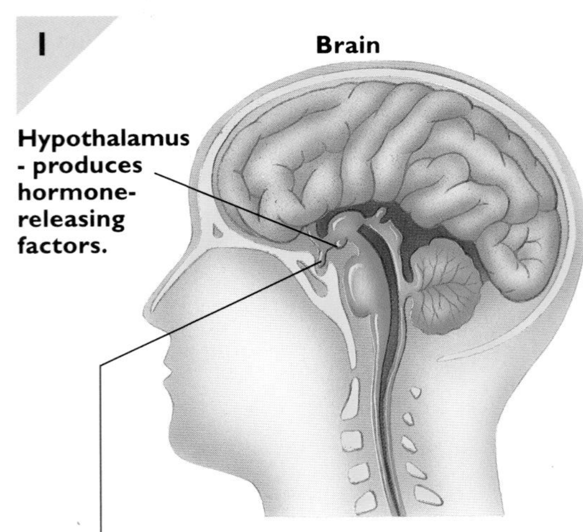


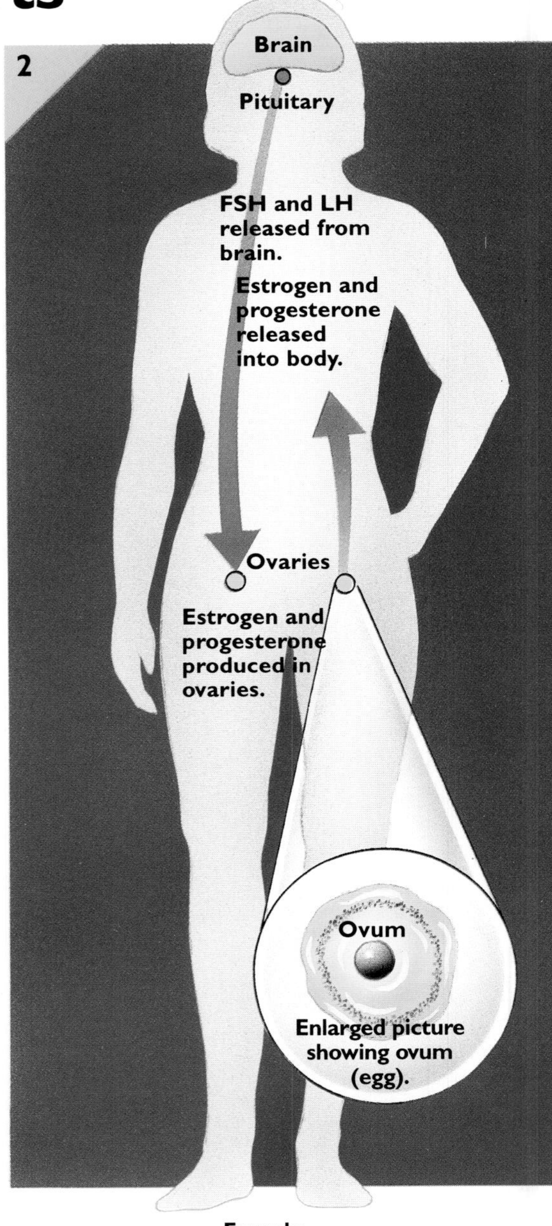


Puberty starts in a tiny part of your brain called the hypothalamus. When this is sufficiently developed, it starts sending high levels of hormones to another part of your brain, called the pituitary gland. The hormones from the hypothalamus are known as "releasing factors" because they trigger the pituitary to start releasing higher levels of two other hormones, known as FSH and LH.*

The hormones FSH and LH make the ova which are in girls' ovaries begin to develop and they start sperm production in boys' testicles.

The ovaries and testicles now start producing high levels of hormones of their own. These are the sex hormones. They help the ovaries and testicles themselves to continue maturing and they also bring about other, more obvious changes of puberty, such



*The full names are Follicle Stimulating Hormone and Luteinizing Hormone.*

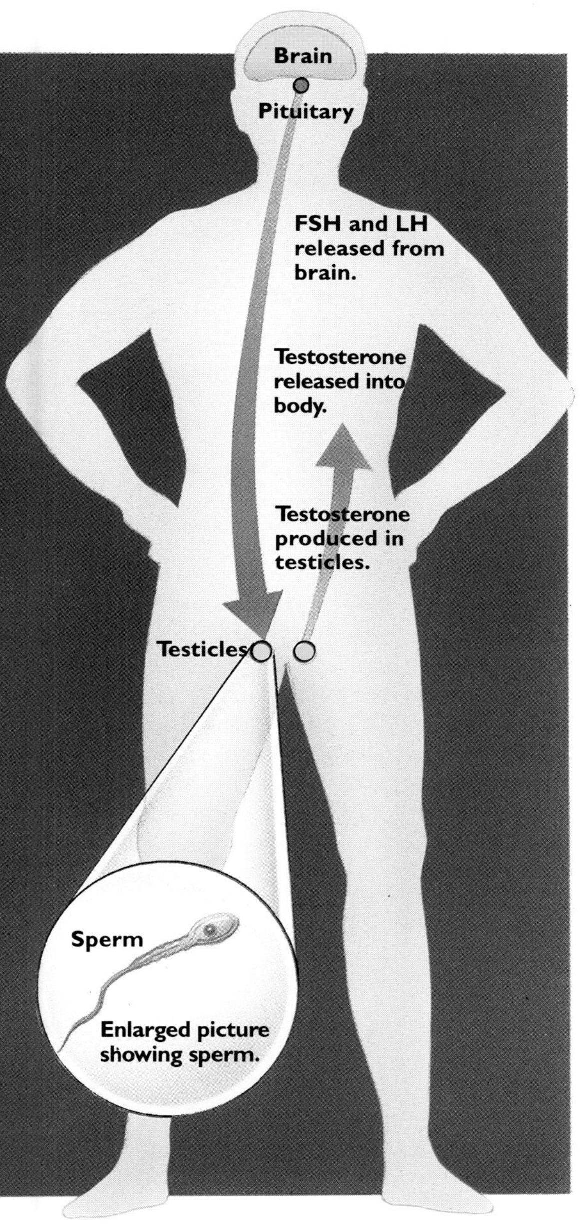


Male

as the development of breasts in girls and the growth of beards in boys. The main female sex hormones are estrogen and progesterone. The most important male sex hormone is testosterone.

The ovaries do not produce only female sex hormones but a low level of male ones as well. In the same way, the testicles produce low levels of female sex hormones in addition to male ones.

*In your body, hormones are in solution and look grayish.

## What are hormones?

This picture shows crystals of the male sex hormone, testosterone, magnified thousands of times.* Many of the changes that take place in males' bodies at puberty are caused by testosterone. There are many other types of hormones in the human body besides those to do with reproduction. Adrenalin, for example, is a hormone which prepares your body to take emergency action when you are feeling afraid or angry.

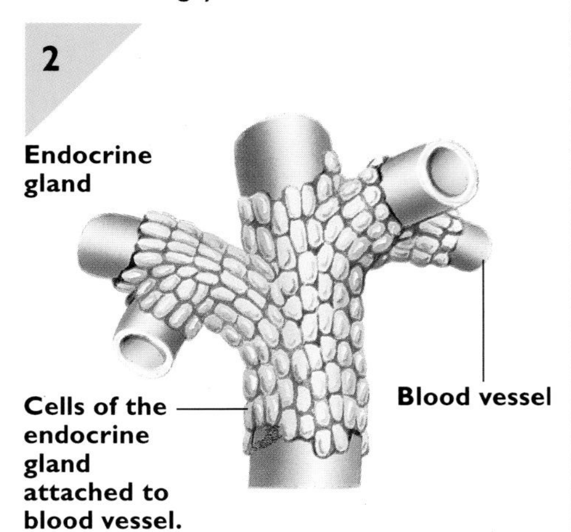


Hormones are produced in your body in groups of cells called endocrine glands. The pituitary, for example, is an endocrine gland. The glands are attached to blood vessels which have thin walls. The hormones pass from the glands through the walls and into your blood. Your blood then carries them all around your body. Different hormones act on different parts of your body.

# Hair

You grow hair on various parts of your body at puberty. Human beings are related to apes and the hair dates from a time when people were covered all over with fairly thick hair. Hair growth at puberty is triggered by the sex hormones. The amount of hair you get depends on what you have inherited from your parents.*

## Pubic hair

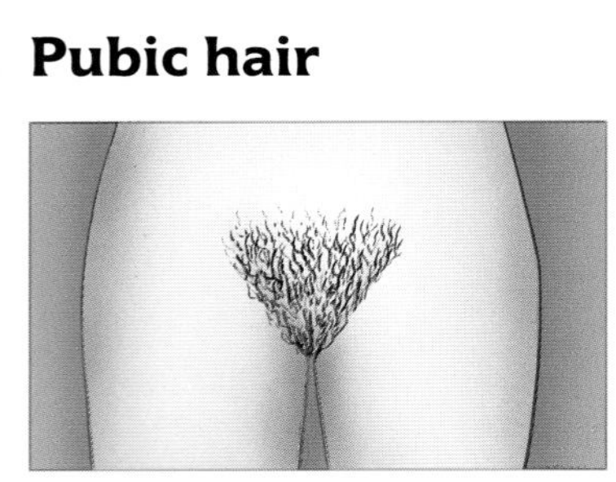

**Female pubic hair**

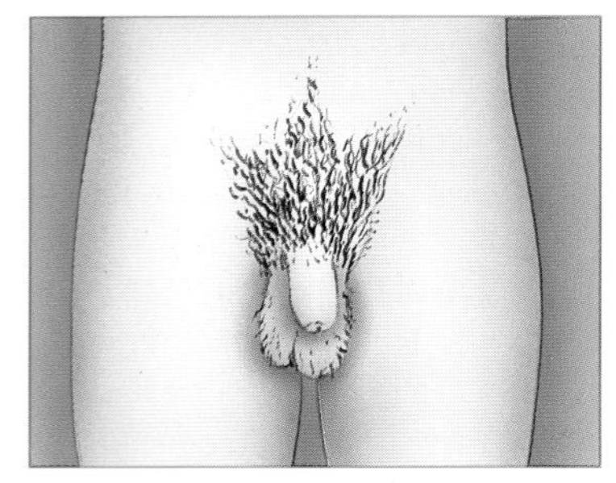

**Male pubic hair**

This is the hair which grows in the area of your external sex organs, or "genitals", at puberty. The hair may help to cushion the pubic bone beneath it and it is also a secondary sexual feature. Although it is not essential for reproduction, it is generally attractive to the opposite sex.

When it first starts to grow, pubic hair is fairly soft, but it eventually becomes coarser than the hair on your head and curly. It is not unusual for pubic hair to be a completely different shade from the hair on your head.

## Underarm hair

You usually start to get hair under your arms a year or two after your pubic hair begins to grow. No one really knows what purpose the hair has.

In some countries many women remove the hair, though there is no medical reason for this. You will not sweat any less and the hair soon grows back again. If you do want to remove it, you can use a razor or special hair-removing cream. Be sure to follow the instructions with the cream carefully, as the skin under your arms is very sensitive.

## Hair on your body

Both males and females get hair on their arms and legs at puberty. Males in particular often get it on their chests too and sometimes on their abdomen, shoulders, back, hands and feet. Body hair shows up more on men than women because it is coarser. If your hair is dark, it will show up more than if it is fair.

Having a lot of hair does not make a man more "manly" or a woman in any way "unwomanly" and it has nothing to do with sexual ability. Although the hair is natural and normal, some people like to shave or use cream to remove it, especially from their legs. It is worth bearing in mind that the hair will grow back again, probably thicker and coarser than it was before.



**You can find out about the hair on your head on page 42.*

## Beards

The growth of a beard and mustache is usually one of the last changes to happen to boys at puberty. First, hair grows on your upper lip, then on your cheeks and lastly on your chin. A lot of men have small hairless patches at the sides of their chin.

At first, the hair is soft but it gradually gets coarser. It is not necessarily the same shade as the hair on your head. Some experts think that men's beards are the equivalent of roosters' combs and that they are an important secondary sexual feature.

## Shaving

Some boys feel slightly embarrassed when their beard begins to grow but you don't have to wait for a thick growth before you start shaving. On the other hand, you don't have to shave. If you decide to let your beard grow, make sure you keep it clean.

The quickest, most convenient way to shave is with an electric razor but many men find they get a closer shave using foam and warm water and a non-electric razor. It is easier to cut yourself this way though. Most men tend to shave in the way shown here.

**Start at an ear and work around to chin. Shave downward in direction of hairs or it may hurt.**

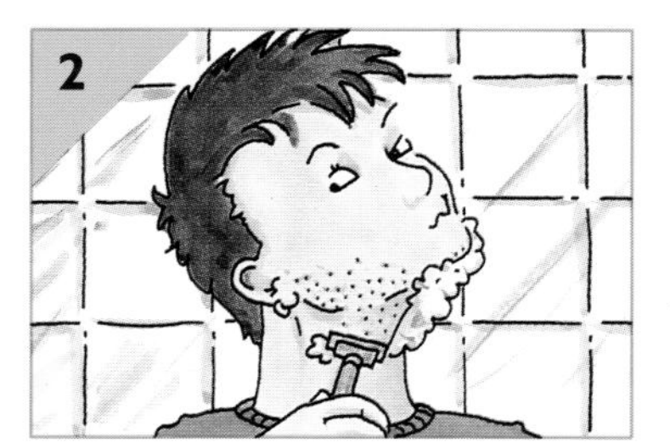


**Do other side of face, top lip, then under chin. For a closer shave, then try shaving upward.**

If you find shaving makes your skin slightly sore, try dabbing on talcum powder when you have finished.

Shaving in warm water opens up the pores of your skin. Splashing on cold water when you have finished helps to close them up again. Aftershave lotion contains astringents, which do the same thing. They also sting when you first put the lotion on. Too much aftershave can make your skin dry and flaky.

It is unhygienic to use anyone else's razor (see also page 44).

## Girls and facial hair

Many girls also get a fine covering of hair on their faces. It is not usually noticeable. If the hair is dark and you are unhappy about it, you can use cream to remove it or ask a beauty therapist about bleaching it. Don't try to shave, as the skin is more sensitive than boys' skin.

## Stray hairs

You can find stray hairs growing anywhere on your body. Some people like to pluck them out or cut them off, especially if they are on their face. It is better not to pluck a hair which is growing out of a mole; just cut the hair instead.

# Breasts

Developing breasts is one of the main changes of puberty for girls. The hormone estrogen, produced by the ovaries, makes the breasts develop, starting usually around age 11. Your nipples are the first things to grow.

As your breasts develop and enlarge, they may feel uncomfortable at times. Also, one breast may develop faster than the other. They will even out later, though no one's breasts match exactly.

The age your breasts start developing has no bearing on their eventual size. Full breast size is usually reached around age 17.

## What are breasts made of?

The breast in this picture is drawn so that you can see what it is made of and how it works.

**1**

When a woman has a baby, a hormone from her pituitary gland triggers milk production in these parts of her breasts. The milk is made from substances which pass out of the woman's blood as it travels through her breasts.

**2**

Each breast contains between 15 and 20 of these tubes or "ducts". In childhood, the ducts are very small but at puberty they enlarge and branch out. When milk is produced in the breasts after a woman has had a baby, it drains into these ducts and is stored there until the baby needs it.

**3**

The nipple is the most sensitive part of the breast. When it is stimulated by sensations such as touch or cold, tiny muscles around its base make it erect.

The shape of nipples varies. It is not unusual for the nipples to be turned inward instead of outward.

When a baby sucks at its mother's breast, a hormone from her pituitary allows the milk to flow out of the ducts through microscopic holes in the nipple.

## What are breasts for?

The main purpose of breasts is to produce milk for feeding any babies a woman might have. They are also an important secondary sexual feature. They are attractive to men and are sensitive to touch, which increases the woman's sexual pleasure.

**4**

The area around the nipple is called the areola. It varies from pink to dark brown in shade, becoming darker as you get older and during pregnancy.

The tiny lumps in the areola are glands. During breast-feeding, these produce a fatty substance which helps to protect the nipples.

Stray hairs often grow in the areola. You can pluck these out or cut them off if you want to.

**5**

As the milk-collecting ducts enlarge at puberty, fat is formed to provide a protective cushion for them. It is the amount of fat in your breasts which determines their size.

**6**

The ducts are separated from each other by elastic fibers. These tend to stretch as you get older, which makes the breasts begin to droop.

## Breast size

A lot of women worry that their breasts are too big or too small. Like worries about general body shape, this may be due to images of "ideal" women given in the media. In reality, all sizes are equally able to feed babies, as the size is determined by fat, not by the milk-producing or storing areas. Breasts are also equally sensitive, whatever their size, and men differ as to the size and shape they find most attractive.

## Boys and breasts

Some boys find that their breasts become tender or swell slightly at puberty. This is nothing to worry about. You are not changing sex and the "breasts" will disappear within about 18 months, as hormone production settles down.

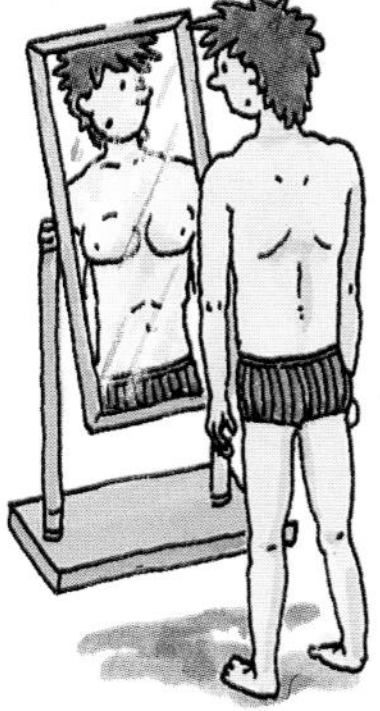

## Bras

Whether or not you wear a bra is up to you. If you are comfortable without one, there is no medical reason for wearing one. The way the elastic fibers stretch and your breasts droop as you get older is quite natural, and wearing a bra will not prevent it. The weight of large breasts can sometimes tear the fibers or stretch them prematurely, though, so if you have large breasts it may be a good idea to wear a bra most of the time. Most women find it more comfortable to wear a bra for doing exercises or sports.

## Buying a bra

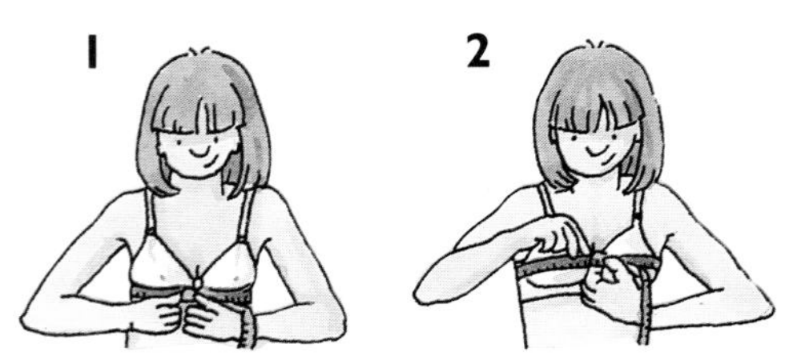


When you buy a bra, you need to give your chest measurement and cup size.

1. To find out your chest size, measure just under your breasts around your ribcage and add 12cm (5in).
   e.g. 68cm (27in) + 12cm (5in) = size 80cm (32in).

2. To find out your cup size, measure again around the fullest part of your breasts. If this is the same as the measurement above, you are an A cup; if there is a 2.5cm (1in) difference, you are a B cup; a 5cm (2in) difference means you are a C cup.

## Do exercises work?

No amount of exercising can increase your breast size, because exercise works by building up muscle and there are no muscles in breasts.

Exercise involving the chest muscles, such as swimming, will strengthen these muscles and may help them to support your breasts more easily.

# Female sex organs

The growth and development of the sex organs is really the major change of puberty. It is what eventually enables you to have children. Girls are often unaware of the changes in their sex organs, because most of them are inside their body.

The picture on the opposite page shows the female sex organs which are outside the body. You can find out about the female sex organs inside the body on pages 18-19 and about the male sex organs on pages 24-25.

External sex organs are called genitals. Girls' genitals are less obvious than boys'.

Vulva: the female genitals are called the vulva, which is the Latin word for opening. On the right you can see the different parts. The only way you can really see your vulva is to use a mirror. Don't worry if yours looks different from the one in this picture. Genitals vary from person to person just like any other part of the body.

**1**

Outer labia: these are two thick folds of skin or "lips". They are made of fat and have pubic hair growing on them. They are normally closed over the inner parts of the vulva, protecting them.

**2**

Urinary opening: this is the opening of the urethra, which is the tube leading from your bladder to the outside of your body. It is where your urine comes out.

**3**

Mons: this is a mound of fat which cushions and protects the pubic bone beneath it. Your pubic hair grows over it.

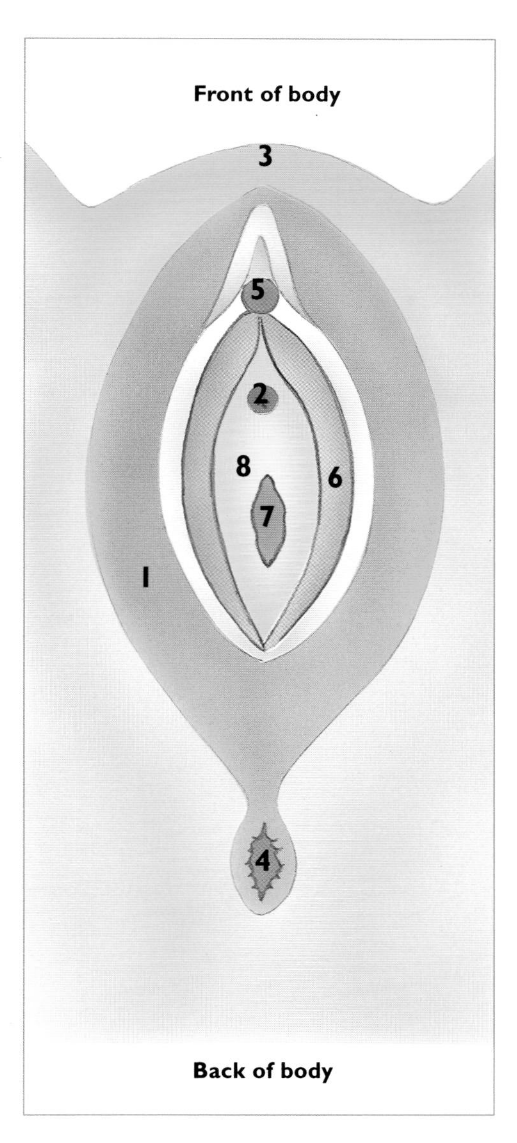


**4**

Anus: this is the hole at the end of your digestive tract where solid waste leaves your body when you go to the toilet.

**5**

Clitoris: this is the most sensitive part of the female body. It is the equivalent of the male's penis, although it is only about the size of a pea. The exact size varies from woman to woman and is not related to sensitivity. Only the tip of the clitoris is visible. This has a fold of skin or "hood" over it, formed by the inner labia meeting at the front of the vulva.

**6**

Inner labia: these are thinner than the outer labia and have no hair on them. As you grow up, they become increasingly sensitive to touch. A lubricating fluid is produced by glands in the labia. The left and right labia are rarely the same size. Sometimes the inner labia stick out from between the outer labia.

**7**

Vaginal opening: this is the opening to the vagina, which is a tube leading to your internal sex organs. It is where the blood comes out when you have a period (see page 20), where the penis fits during sex (see page 27) and where babies leave the body when they are born. Although the opening is very small, it stretches easily.

**8**

Hymen: this is a thin layer of skin which partially covers the vaginal opening. As your vagina grows and stretches during puberty, the hymen gradually breaks down. It is often broken before puberty, especially if you play a lot of sport. Even if your hymen still seems intact, there will be enough tiny holes in it for period blood to get out.

# Female sex organs inside the body

The picture on the right shows the internal female sex organs seen from the front. Most of them are drawn so that you can see inside. Like the rest of the body, the internal sex organs grow considerably at puberty. The weight of the uterus (womb) may increase by as much as 44g (1½oz), for example.

I

Ovaries: a female has two ovaries. They are low down in her abdomen, one on each side, and are attached to the outside of the uterus by connecting fibers. Fully developed ovaries are about the shape and size of shelled walnuts.

When a girl is born, she already has hundreds of thousands of ova (egg cells) stored in her ovaries. At puberty, the hormones FSH and LH, produced by the pituitary, make the ova begin to mature and be released from the ovaries. Usually, one ovum is released each month, from alternate ovaries. This is called ovulation. The process continues until the age of about 50. The time when it stops is called the menopause.

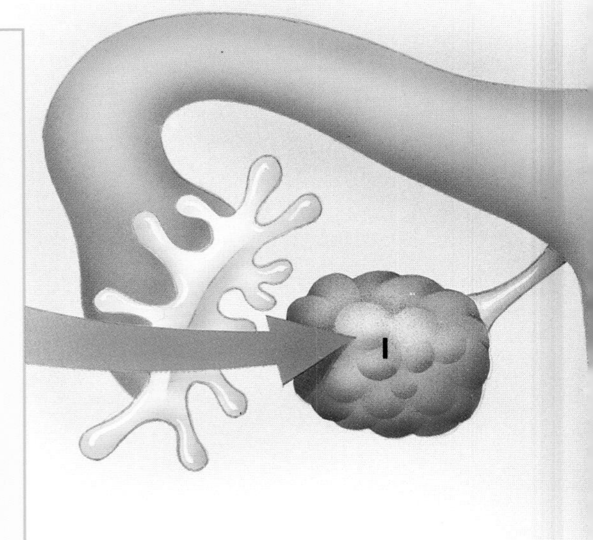


## Where are the internal sex organs?

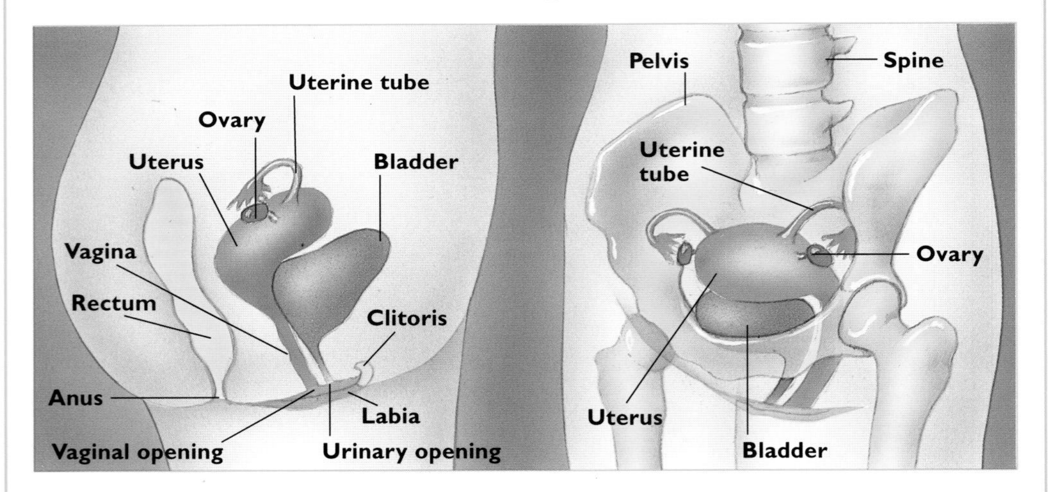


The two pictures above show the position of the female sex organs in the abdomen. The one on the left is a sideways view, so you can see where the organs are in relation to the bladder and rectum (back passage) and how they connect up with the external sex organs described on the previous page. The other picture shows how the organs (especially the uterus) are protected by the bones of the pelvis.

**2**

Uterine tubes: the uterine, or Fallopian, tubes are muscular tubes. They are about 12cm (4¾in) long and the thickness of a pencil. The hollow part is only the width of the lead of a pencil.

When an ovum is released from an ovary, the fringed end of the nearest uterine tube swoops down and draws it into the tube. The muscular walls of the tube and tiny hairs inside it then move the ovum along toward the uterus.

It is while an ovum is in the uterine tube that a woman may become pregnant if she has sex. A sperm cell (from the man's body) may fertilize the ovum. You can find out what this means on page 30.

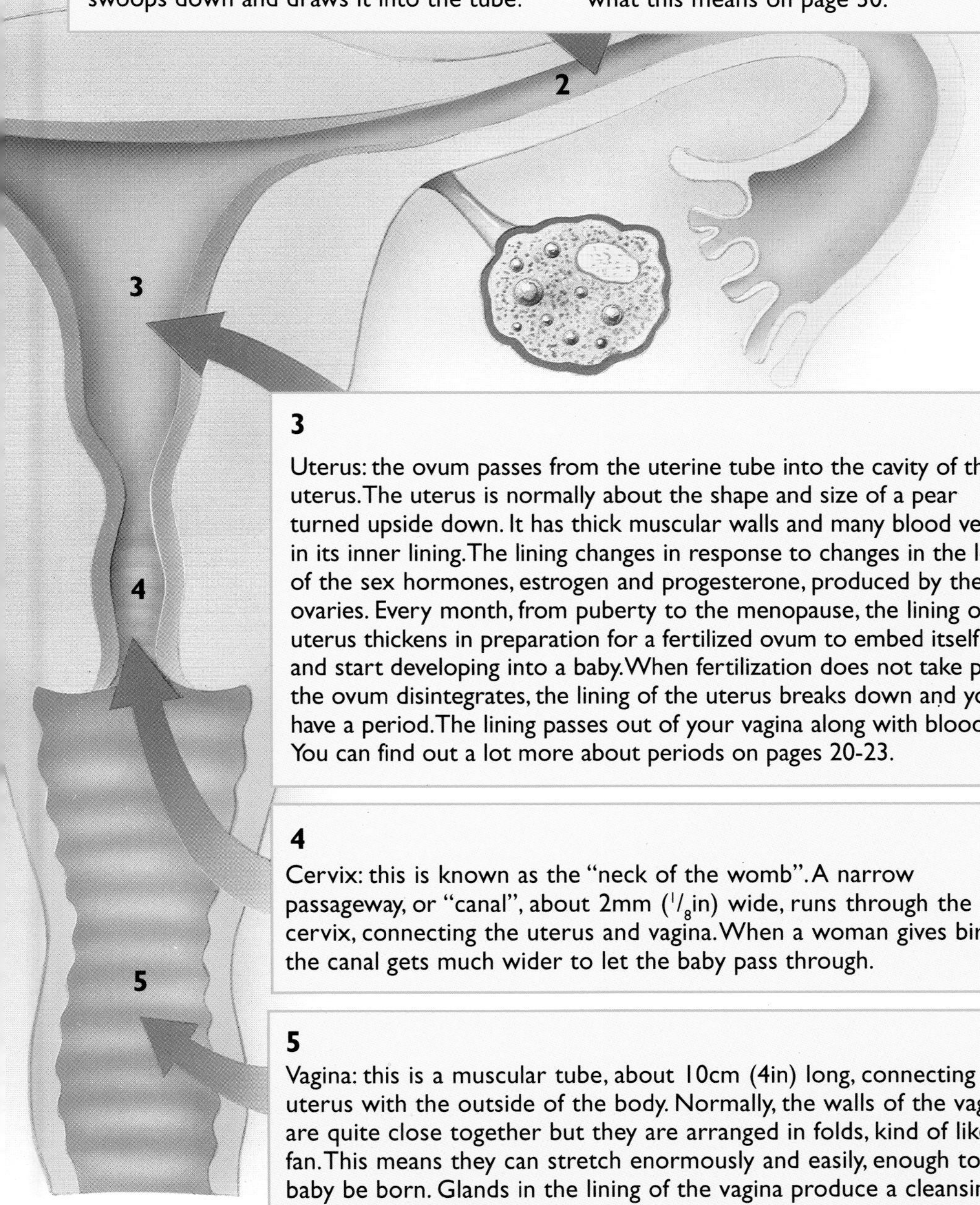

**3**

Uterus: the ovum passes from the uterine tube into the cavity of the uterus. The uterus is normally about the shape and size of a pear turned upside down. It has thick muscular walls and many blood vessels in its inner lining. The lining changes in response to changes in the levels of the sex hormones, estrogen and progesterone, produced by the ovaries. Every month, from puberty to the menopause, the lining of the uterus thickens in preparation for a fertilized ovum to embed itself in it and start developing into a baby. When fertilization does not take place, the ovum disintegrates, the lining of the uterus breaks down and you have a period. The lining passes out of your vagina along with blood. You can find out a lot more about periods on pages 20-23.

**4**

Cervix: this is known as the "neck of the womb". A narrow passageway, or "canal", about 2mm (⅛in) wide, runs through the cervix, connecting the uterus and vagina. When a woman gives birth, the canal gets much wider to let the baby pass through.

**5**

Vagina: this is a muscular tube, about 10cm (4in) long, connecting the uterus with the outside of the body. Normally, the walls of the vagina are quite close together but they are arranged in folds, kind of like a fan. This means they can stretch enormously and easily, enough to let a baby be born. Glands in the lining of the vagina produce a cleansing and lubricating fluid.

# Periods

Starting to have periods is probably the single most important change of puberty for girls. On these two pages you can see how periods come about because the lining of the uterus breaks down and causes a small amount of bleeding from the vagina. This may sound kind of frightening but, if you are prepared for it, it is nothing at all to worry about. The blood trickles out gradually over a few days and good-quality tampons or sanitary pads can easily cope with the flow.

Periods can start any time between the ages of nine and 18, but the most usual time is about a year after your breasts have begun to develop.

## What is a period?

**Many people first notice a period has started when they go to the bathroom.**

You appear to lose only blood when you have a period but the flow really consists of cells from the lining of the uterus, which are simply stained by blood and mixed with a sticky fluid from the cervix. The blood comes from small blood vessels in the uterus which tear as the lining comes away from the walls. On average, you lose about two tablespoons of blood per period. A period can last from two to about eight days but the average is four.

## Hormones and periods

Here you can see how the menstrual cycle is controlled by hormones. The cycle given here is an average one lasting 28 days. Yours may be different.

### Day 1

The period starts. At the same time, the hormone FSH from the pituitary is making an ovum mature in a tiny sac or "follicle" in one of the ovaries.

### Day 5

The period is over. The ovum continues to mature and the follicle moves toward the surface of the ovary. The follicle is producing the hormone estrogen. This makes the lining of the uterus start to thicken again. At the moment it is probably around 1mm ($^{1}/_{16}$ in) thick.

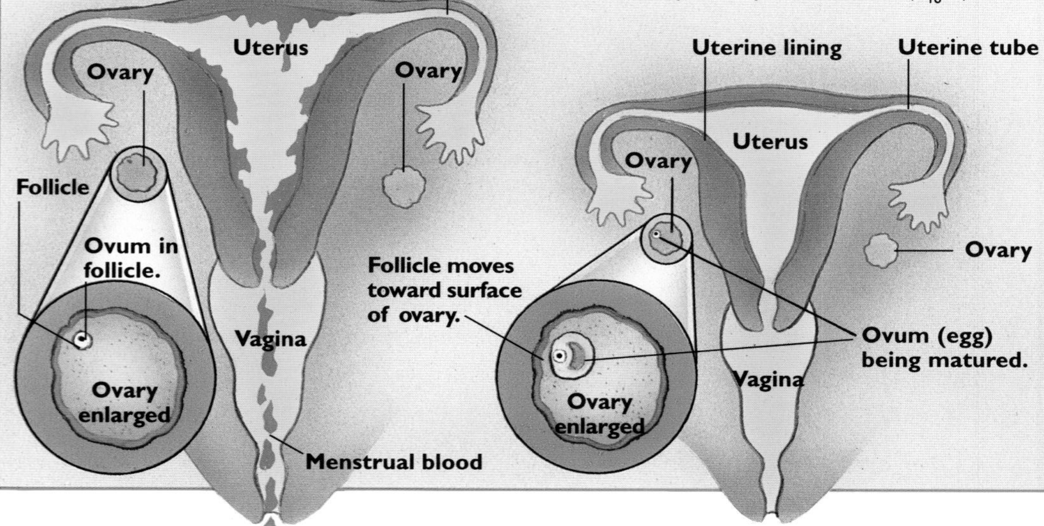

## How often do periods happen?

Another name for periods is menstruation. This comes from the Latin word *mensis*, which means month. On average, a woman has a period about every four weeks (28 days). The cycle can vary, though, from about 20 days to 35 from woman to woman, and even in the same woman from month to month.

## Myths about periods

Over the centuries, there have been many myths about periods. Most date from the time when the cause of them was not understood. Odd superstitions survive even today, such as you should not wash your hair when you have a period, or eat ice cream. In reality, a woman can do everything she normally does, including taking a bath or shower, and swimming.

### Day 14

The pituitary stops producing FSH and produces LH instead. This makes the now mature ovum burst out of its follicle, leave the ovary (ovulation) and enter the uterine tube. The empty follicle, known as the "yellow body", starts to produce the second female sex hormone, progesterone. Progesterone makes the thickening lining of the uterus soft and spongy so that if the ovum is fertilized, it can embed itself.

### Day 21

The ovum has been in the uterus for a few days now. If it has not been fertilized, both it and the yellow body start to disintegrate and the levels of estrogen and progesterone fall. By this time, the lining of the uterus is about 5mm (¼ in) thick. It starts to disintegrate and come away from the walls of the uterus. Some of the blood vessels kink and tear in the process. On day 1, the next period starts and the cycle begins again.

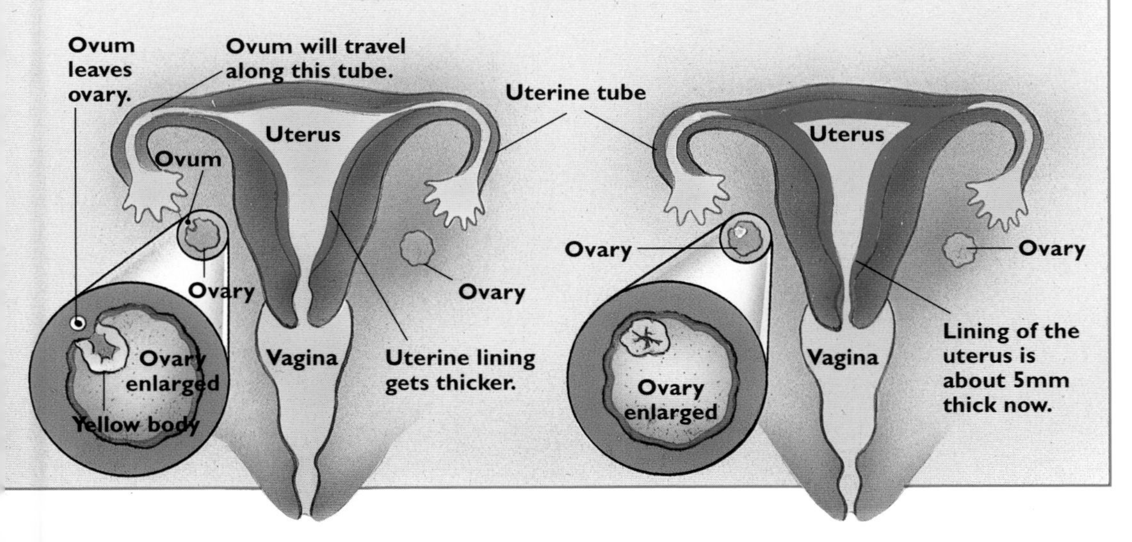

## What to wear

You have a choice of using either sanitary pads or tampons to absorb menstrual blood. Pads soak up the blood as it leaves your body from the vaginal opening, whereas tampons fit right inside the vagina and catch it before it leaves your body. Both pads and tampons are fairly expensive. You may see free samples offered in magazine advertisements. It is worth sending off for these, so you can decide which type and make you prefer.

## Pads

These come in different sizes and thicknesses so you can choose one to match the shape of your body and the heaviness of your period.

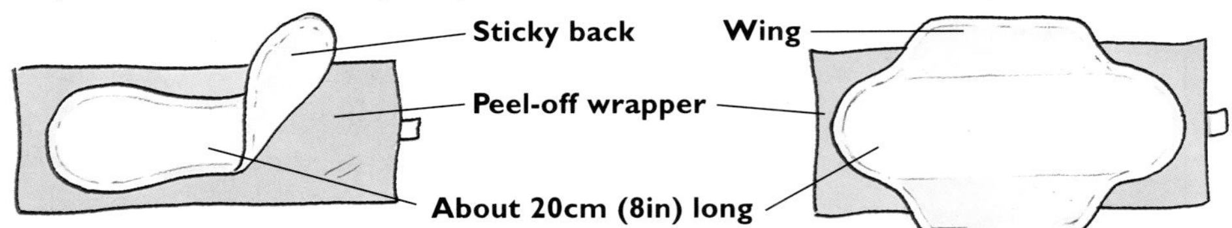


"Press-on" pads have a sticky stripe on the back which you press to your underwear to hold the pad in place. These are comfortable enough, though occasionally they can crease up or come slightly unstuck.

Some pads have side flaps or "wings", as well as a sticky stripe on the back. The flaps stick to the underside of your underwear to hold the pad in place extra firmly. They also make the pads more absorbent.

## Changing pads

It is best to change your pad every few hours, even if your flow is not heavy. Menstrual blood is perfectly clean, but once outside your body it meets bacteria from the air and this can cause a smell or even an infection.

Flushing pads down the toilet can block the pipes and is not good for the environment. It is better to put them in a paper or plastic bag and throw them in the trash can. You can always carry a few bags with you when you go out for any length of time. Paper bags are sometimes provided in public restrooms.

## Problems with periods

Menstruation is a normal, healthy process, not an illness, and many women have no problems at all with periods. On the other hand, the female hormone cycle is very complex. Whereas a male's sex hormone levels remain more or less the same from day to day, a female's are changing every day over the course of her cycle. The hormones are carried in your bloodstream, so they can affect other parts of your body besides your sex organs. This makes some people feel kind of funny before or during their period.

## Painful periods

Quite a lot of women get an ache or cramp-like pains in their lower abdomen at the start of a period. Doctors think this is caused by hormones making the muscles of the uterus contract (get smaller). If the pain is only slight, exercise can help. If it is very bad, you may need to take a painkiller and lie down with a hot water bottle. The medical name for period pain is dysmenorrhea.*

*Pronounced dis-men-or-ear.

## Tampons

Many women prefer tampons to pads for various reasons. Once a tampon is in the right position in your vagina, you cannot feel it at all. You do not need to worry about people seeing the shape of a pad through close-fitting clothes, or be concerned about any smell. You can take a bath or go swimming. Tampons are easier to carry around because they are smaller.

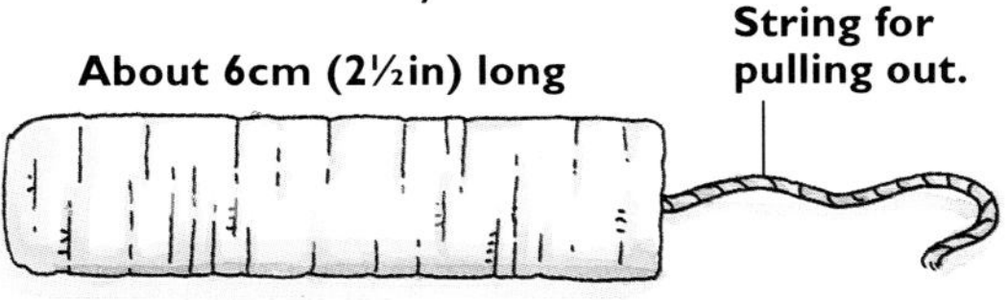


## Changing tampons

It is not as easy to tell when a tampon needs to be changed as it is a pad, though you can sometimes feel a bubbling sensation just before the tampon starts to leak and the string may become bloodstained. You should change tampons every four to six hours anyway and, if you use them at night, as soon as you wake up in the morning. If you leave them in too long, bacteria in the vagina may cause infection. One type of infection, though rare, can be very serious.

Tampons will flush down the toilet but it is better for the environment if you dispose of them in the same way as pads (see opposite page).

## Inserting a tampon

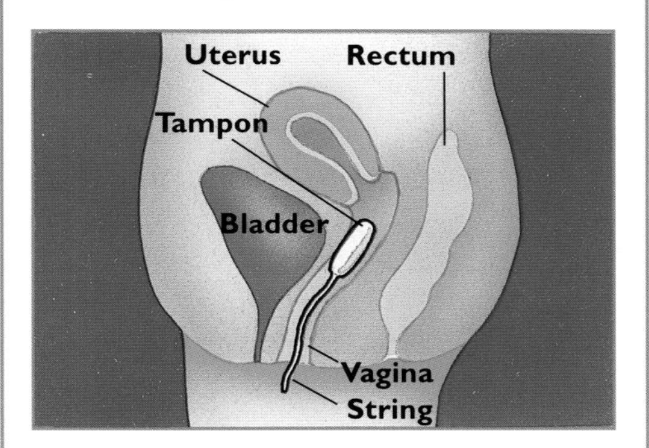


Some girls do not want to try tampons when they first start their periods, but there is no reason not to, if you feel like it. Start with the smallest size; you can always go on to larger ones if they cannot cope with your flow. Tampons come with instructions and you should read and follow these very carefully. The best time to try inserting a tampon for the first time is when your flow is heaviest. Always wash your hands before unwrapping a tampon to guard against infection and if you drop one on the floor, don't use it. If you can't get a tampon in, it probably means that your hymen is still fairly intact. Try again in a few months, when it may have broken more.

## Premenstrual tension (PMT)

Some women suffer from PMT for a few days before a period. PMT, also known as PMS (premenstrual syndrome), is probably caused by changing hormone levels. Symptoms include sore breasts, a bloated, heavy feeling especially in the abdomen, headaches, pimples, and feeling tired, irritable or depressed. There is no proven medical remedy but your doctor should be able to give you some tips.

## Irregular periods

This is not necessarily a problem. It is quite usual for periods to be irregular for the first year or two. This is because your hormones are not yet in a regular rhythm. You may even find that several months pass between periods. Other reasons for periods becoming irregular include being ill, feeling upset, worried or stressed, and even just changing your routine.

**28 days is the average cycle, but yours may be longer or shorter.**

# Male sex organs

It is easy for a boy to tell when his sex organs are developing because they increase visibly in size. The testicles start to get bigger and the penis follows about a year later. The picture on the right shows the male sex organs viewed from the front. They are drawn so that you can see the different parts.

**1**

Testicles: the male's testicles are the equivalent of the female's ovaries. They produce male sex cells (sperm) and the male sex hormone, testosterone. The testicles are about the size of small plums. The left testicle usually hangs lower than the right. From puberty on, sperm cells are formed continuously in tiny, coiled tubes inside the testicles. It takes over two months for a sperm to be formed. Several million sperm complete the process every day. Unlike the ovaries, the testicles do not stop producing sex cells during middle age. Production continues, though at a lower level, right into old age.

**2**

Scrotum: the testicles are contained in a loose pouch of wrinkled skin called the scrotum. They are outside the abdomen, as sperm are only produced at a temperature around 2°C (4°F) lower than normal internal body temperature. When your testicles are exposed to cold, the skin of your scrotum shrinks, drawing them closer to your body for warmth.

## Position of the sex organs

This picture shows the male sex organs viewed from the right.

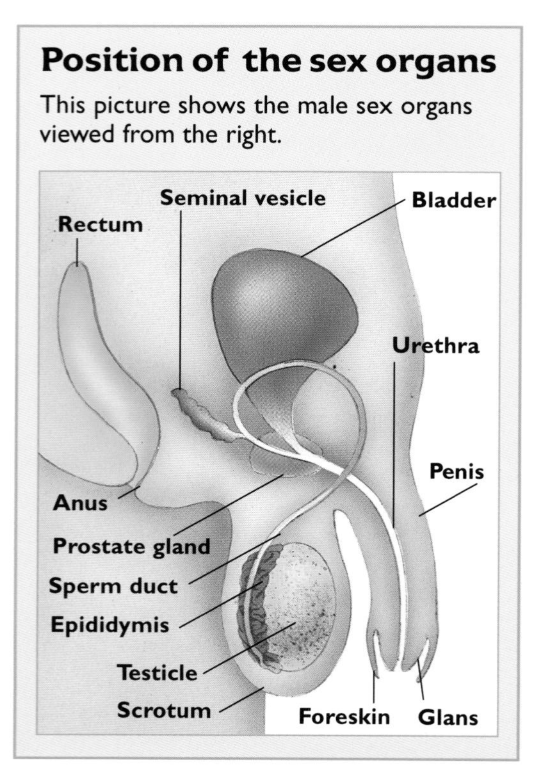


**3**

Epididymis: the epididymis is a coiled tube which lies over the back of each testicle. Each tube would be 6m (20ft) long if it was uncoiled. The sperm cells are squeezed from the testicles into the epididymis, where they mature for about two weeks.

**4**

Sperm ducts: these are two tubes, about 40cm (16in) long, which lead from the epididymis up into the pelvis. There, they join into the urethra as it leaves the bladder. The tubes are muscular and about the thickness of string. The sperm travel along the tubes from the epididymis toward the penis.

**5**

Seminal vesicles: these are glands. They produce a nourishing fluid which helps to give the sperm energy.

**6**

Prostate gland: this is about the size of a walnut and produces a fluid which helps the sperm to move.

**7**

Urethra: this is longer in males than females and has two functions. One is to carry urine to the outside of the body. During sexual excitement it carries semen, which is the mixture of sperm and the fluids produced by the seminal vesicles and the prostate gland.

**8**

Penis: usually the penis is fairly small and soft. During sexual excitement, more blood flows into it than usual, and less flows out, so it becomes larger and harder and stands away from the body (an erection). This enables it to fit inside the female's vagina. Sperm can be deposited in the vagina so that a baby can be made.

**9**

Glans: this is the name for the tip of the penis, which is the most sensitive part.

**10**

Foreskin: this is the fold of skin which covers the glans of the penis. Glands under the foreskin produce a white, creamy substance called smegma. This helps the skin to slide back smoothly over the glans.

## Circumcision

In some religions, for example the Jewish one, it is customary to cut away a boy's foreskin surgically a few days after birth. This is called circumcision. In some countries, such as the USA, the operation is routinely performed because it is believed to be more hygienic. When the foreskin is intact, smegma can collect beneath it, causing a smell or occasionally an infection. However, if you roll back your foreskin and wash gently underneath it every day, you will probably avoid this problem.

## Penis size

The size of unerect penises varies from male to male and has no relation to body size. Some boys worry about having a small penis. In fact, small penises generally increase their size a lot more than large ones when they become erect, so that apparent differences become much less. The average length of an erect penis is between 12½ and 17½cm (5 and 6¾in). A smaller erect penis does not make any difference to either the male's or female's sexual pleasure.

# Sex

As the level of your sex hormones increases and your sex organs mature, you gradually become more aware of sexual feelings. This may start with an increased awareness of your own body and emotions, which develops to include a new interest in the opposite sex. At first, this often takes the form of dreams and fantasies. Later, it becomes a desire for physical contact and ultimately for sexual intercourse.

In many countries, sexual intercourse is illegal under a certain age. In the US, the age varies from state to state. This does not mean that once you have reached the age of consent, you have to have sexual intercourse. You should not let anyone pressure you into it before you feel completely ready and have considered all the possible consequences. These include unwanted pregnancy and disease, for example AIDS (see pages 28, 30-33 and 44).

## Touching, stroking and kissing

Most people have quite a lot of physical contact of a nonsexual kind with their family and close friends, which may involve touching and kissing. The line between sexual and nonsexual contact is not a clear one.

The areas of the body that are the most sexually sensitive are called the erogenous zones. These include the genitals, lips, breasts and buttocks, but ear lobes, feet and many other areas are sensitive in different people.

"Making out", "petting" and "necking" are all slang words which are used to describe sexual kissing, touching and stroking. The erogenous zones tend to be touched most.

4

Sexual contact often involves touching or stroking areas of another person's body that you would not normally touch, such as the breasts or genitals. Deep kissing on the lips, sometimes called "French kissing", when one or both partners put their tongue in the other's mouth, also frequently forms a part of sexual contact.

Sexual touching and kissing of this kind usually create a feeling of intense pleasure in both partners and may lead to a desire for sexual intercourse.

No one has the right to force or persuade someone into having sexual contact with them. Everyone has the right to say "no".

## Sexual intercourse

1. Strictly speaking, sexual intercourse begins when a male's penis enters a female's vagina, and ends when it is withdrawn. However, intercourse, or "making love", is almost always preceded by a period of touching, stroking and kissing which is known as "foreplay".

2. Once the penis is inside the vagina, one or both partners move their pelvis, so that it slides in and out repeatedly. This creates a sensation of pleasure.

This stage can last from a few minutes to over an hour, with changes of rhythm and rest periods.

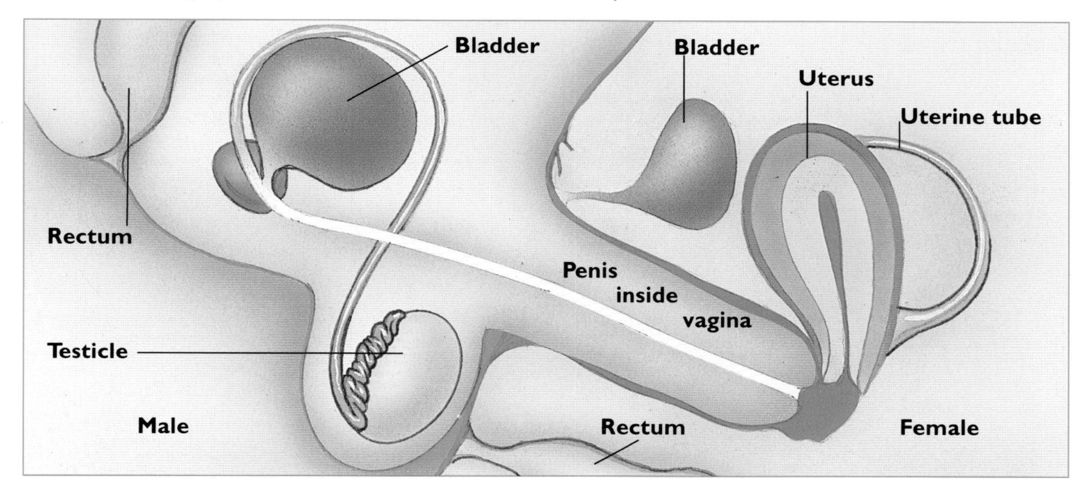


3. Eventually, because of the stimulation to the penis and the clitoris, orgasm usually occurs.

This is the climax of sexual excitement both for males and females. It is often called "coming". An orgasm consists of a series of brief muscular spasms (contractions) in the sex organs. These are felt as a throbbing or pulsating sensation, which spreads through the whole body, and cause a feeling of intense pleasure followed by a feeling of relaxation.

One partner may reach orgasm before the other, or a couple may have their orgasms at the same time. Orgasm may not occur every time, especially in females. In males, semen is squirted (ejaculated) out of the penis by the muscular contractions.

## Changes in the body

Sexual excitement brings about a whole range of changes in the body.

In women's bodies, glands in the vagina produce a lubricating fluid, so that the penis can enter it more easily. The breasts may get larger and the nipples become erect.

In men's bodies, the penis becomes larger and harder, and points upward at an angle away from the body (an erection), enabling it to fit into the vagina. The testicles swell and are drawn closer to the body.

In both sexes, muscles all over the body become tense, the heart beats faster, blood pressure rises and breathing becomes faster and shallow. The chest (especially in females) and the face may become flushed.

## Ejaculation

The semen that is ejaculated from the penis at orgasm is a mixture of sperm (male sex cells) and fluids produced by the prostate gland and the seminal vesicles (see page 25).

On average, only a teaspoonful of semen comes out of the penis with each ejaculation, but this contains hundreds of millions of sperm.

The muscular contractions of orgasm squeeze the sperm from their storage place near the testicles, through the sperm ducts to the urethra, which leads from the bladder through the middle of the penis. Muscles around the base of the bladder act as a valve and ensure that urine cannot pass down the urethra at the same time as semen.

## Sex and emotions

Sex is not just about physical sensations; it usually involves very strong emotions as well. How people feel about it usually depends a great deal on how emotionally involved they are with their partner and on how much they trust them.

Problems with sex often have emotional causes. Anxiety, shyness, fear and unhappiness can all have physical effects on the body.

One of the few occasions when a problem with sex is likely to be purely physical is if a woman experiences slight pain and bleeding when the penis pierces the hymen* the first time she has intercourse. (In many women, the hymen has been stretched or broken before this by playing sports or using tampons.)

## Sex and pregnancy

Once a girl has started ovulating (releasing eggs) and having periods, there is always a chance that sexual intercourse could make her pregnant, unless special precautions are taken to prevent a baby from starting. These precautions are known as contraception (meaning "against conception"). On pages 30-33, you can find out about the contraceptive methods used to prevent pregnancy.

## Homosexuality

Homosexuality means being sexually attracted only to people of your own sex. *Homo* comes from the Greek word meaning "the same". (Heterosexuals are people who are sexually attracted to the opposite sex; *heteros* is the Greek word for "other".) Female homosexuality is usually called lesbianism.

It is common, and quite normal, to experience strong feelings for someone of the same sex, especially during puberty. Such feelings at puberty usually give way to strong attraction to the opposite sex.

It is thought that about one in ten people are homosexual or "gay" into adulthood. Many more people are bisexual, which means they are attracted to both sexes.

No one really knows why some people are attracted to their own sex, while others are not.

## Sexually transmitted diseases (STDs)

These are also known as venereal diseases (VD). They are infections in the sex organs caused by microbes (microscopic living creatures) which are passed from one person's body to another's during sexual contact.

There are many different types of STDs. Some affect both sexes; some affect only males and some only females. A few can develop without sexual contact.

The first symptoms of many of the diseases are similar. They can include itching or soreness of the genitals or anus; a discharge; a sore, lump or rash near the genitals or anus; and pain when going to the bathroom.

One of the problems with STDs is that people can sometimes have a disease and infect a partner without knowing it, because they have no symptoms.

Almost all STDs can be cured if they are treated early enough by a doctor. One very important exception to this is AIDS (see page 44).



*The hymen is described on page 17.

## Fantasies

It is common to fantasize during puberty, especially during masturbation. Some people like to fantasize about someone they know, or about famous people, such as pop stars or actors. Others make up imaginary characters. You may be surprised or troubled at the form some of your fantasies take. This is normal. Fantasies give you the opportunity to imagine doing things that might be unacceptable if you were actually to do them.

## Masturbation

Masturbation means handling the genitals to give sexual pleasure, either to yourself or to someone else.

Males generally masturbate by rubbing the penis rhythmically backward and forward in their hand, while females generally rub the area around the clitoris rhythmically with their fingers. This may eventually lead to an orgasm (see page 27).

There used to be many myths about the bad effects masturbation could have. In fact, masturbation only becomes unhealthy if someone wants to do it all the time.

Males tend to masturbate more than females during puberty. This may be partly because the penis is more accessible than the clitoris and males grow up used to touching it every time they go to the bathroom.

## Wet dreams

These are common in boys during puberty. While you are asleep, you have an erection and ejaculate semen. This happens while you are dreaming, though not necessarily about sex. It is nothing to worry about: your body is just getting used to its new way of working.

If you feel embarrassed about staining the sheets, you can sponge the stain out with soap and cold water, or keep tissues or toilet paper near the bed for mopping up.

## Embarrassing erections

Most males are embarrassed by having erections at inconvenient moments during puberty. Most erections are triggered by a sexual thought, for example when you see a girl you like. Some happen when your genitals are accidentally stimulated, for example by the vibrations of a moving train. The best way to make the erections subside is to concentrate very hard on something else.

It is very common for males to wake up with an erection in the morning. This is due to dreaming, though not necessarily about sex.

# Contraception

The moment when a woman becomes pregnant after having sexual intercourse is called conception or fertilization. There are various measures a couple can take to prevent pregnancy. This is called contraception (against conception). Some methods of contraception are more effective than others. In many states they are provided free and in confidence through special family planning clinics.

## Conception

When a male ejaculates semen inside a female's vagina during intercourse, hundreds of millions of sperm cells are deposited close to the cervix. From there, sperm swim up through the uterus and into the uterine tubes. Only about a thousand sperm get as far as the tubes before they die. If there is an ovum in one of the tubes, the sperm cluster around it and one sperm may join with it. This is conception or fertilization. Together, the ovum and sperm make one new cell. This grows and develops into a baby in the female's uterus.

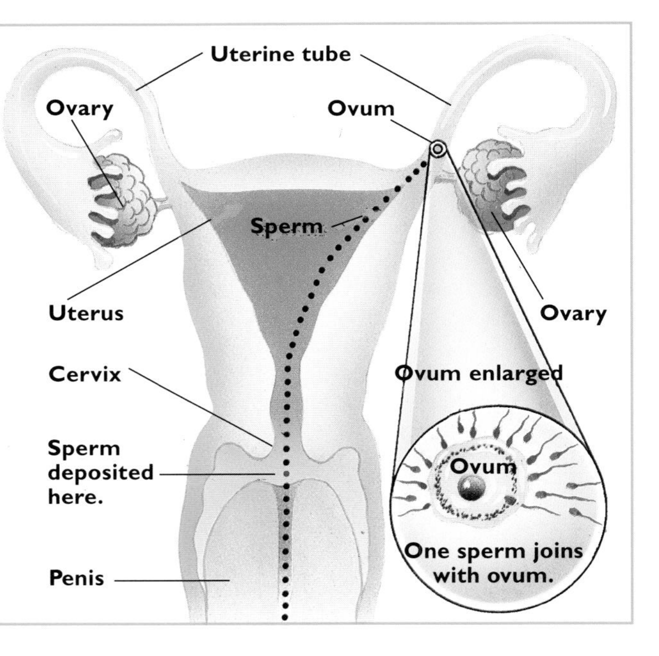


## Combined pill

Some women put on weight.

This is one of the most effective methods of contraception. The woman takes a pill a day, usually for three weeks in every four. The pills contain estrogen and progestogen (similar to progesterone). They work by lowering the output of the hormones FSH and LH from the woman's pituitary so that no ova mature in her ovaries and ovulation cannot take place.

The pill has to be prescribed by a doctor and the woman has regular checkups to make sure she is not suffering from any side effects. These can include weight gain, headaches, sore breasts and, in very rare cases, high blood pressure or even a thrombosis (blood clot), especially in the legs. A woman is not prescribed the pill in the first place if the doctor thinks she is especially likely to suffer serious side effects.

One good side effect of the pill is that periods become lighter, more regular and more pain-free. For this reason it is sometimes specially prescribed for women who have problems with their periods.

## Progestogen-only pill (POP)

This is only slightly less effective than the combined pill. It is taken every day. The pills contain progestogen only and work by altering the lining of the cervix so that sperm find it difficult to enter the uterus. They also ensure that if an ovum is fertilized, it cannot embed itself. (The combined pill does these things too, as well as preventing ovulation. The POP also prevents ovulation in some women.) The POP is prescribed by a doctor and the woman has regular checkups. Side effects can include irregular periods, pimples and sore breasts.

## IUD and IUS

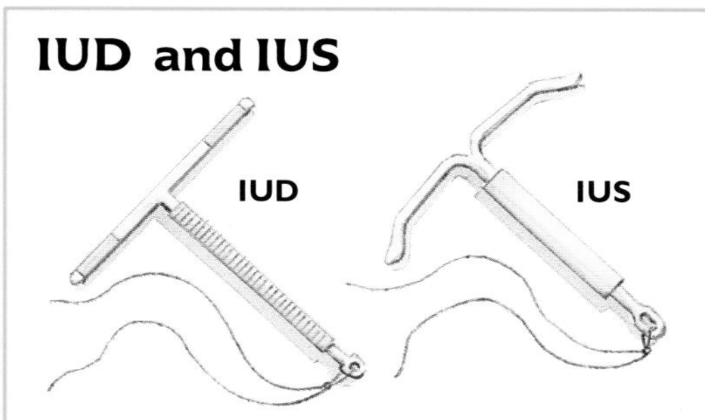


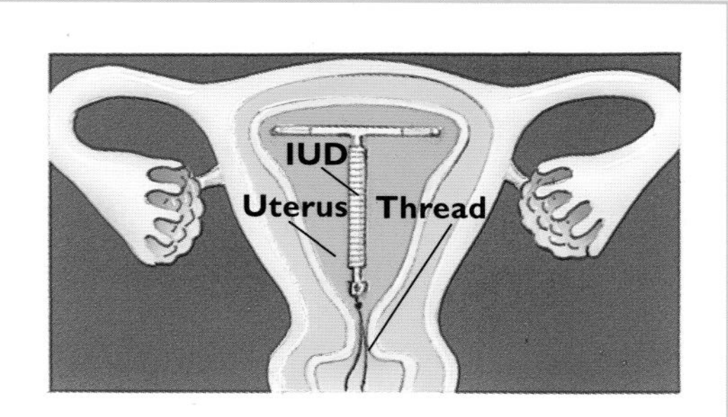


These are two similar methods. An IUD (intrauterine device), which used to be called a coil, is made of plastic and copper; an IUS (intrauterine system) is a plastic device containing progestogen. They are put into a woman's uterus and work mainly by preventing sperm from meeting an ovum.

The IUD or IUS is inserted by a doctor or nurse, through the woman's vagina, and can then be kept in place for a few years, without her being aware of it. She checks regularly that it has not fallen out by feeling for a thread which is left hanging down into her vagina. IUDs can cause heavy or painful periods, and increase the risk of infections. With an IUS, periods become lighter but there is a risk of pimples and sore breasts.

## Diaphragms and caps

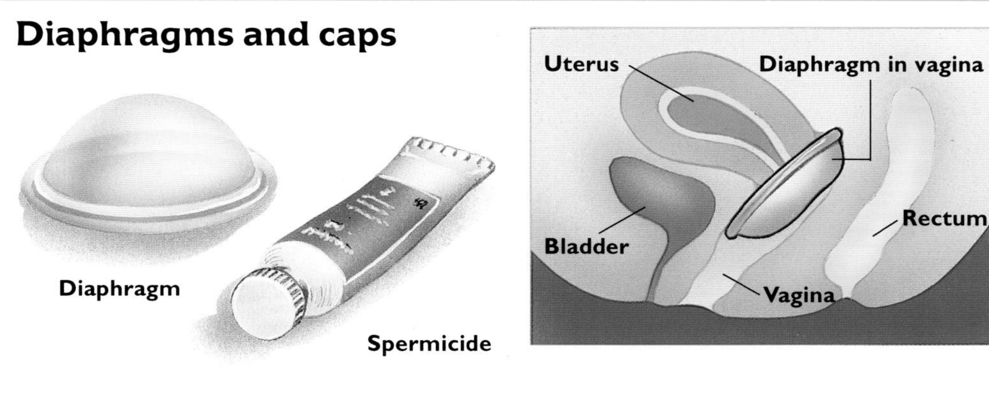


Diaphragms and caps are made of soft rubber. They fit over the cervix and help to prevent sperm from entering the uterus. To be effective, they have to be smeared with a "spermicide". This is a cream or jelly containing special chemicals which help to kill sperm.*

The woman has to be measured for a diaphragm or cap by a doctor or nurse. She then inserts it herself before having intercourse and leaves it in place for several hours afterward, for the spermicide to act. Neither she nor the man can feel the diaphragm or cap during intercourse.

**Spermicides are not effective used on their own.*

## Condoms

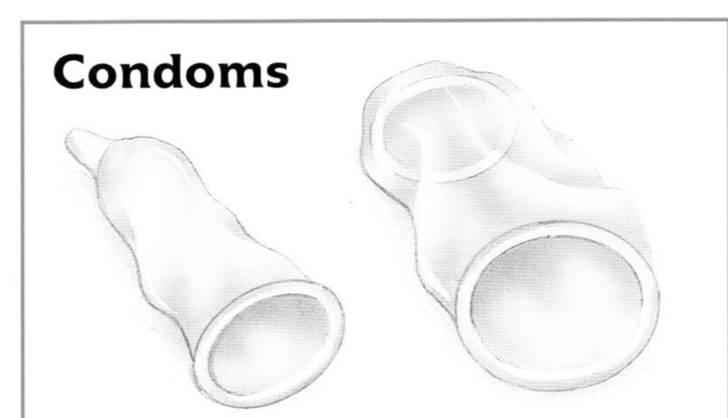

**Male condom** **Female condom**

A male condom (rubber in slang) is a thin rubber sheath which is put onto the man's erect penis before intercourse. When he ejaculates, the semen is caught in the end of the sheath. He has to remove his penis carefully from the vagina soon after ejaculating, or the sheath may slip off as his penis shrinks back to its normal size.

A female condom is a sheath which is put into the vagina to line it and catch the semen. The couple have to be careful that the open end of the condom stays outside the vagina and that the penis enters the condom and not between the condom and the vagina.

Condoms are sold at pharmacies, drugstores and in many other stores. They are also often sold from coin machines in public restrooms. Condoms are the only method of contraception which also helps to prevent the spread of infections, including HIV (see page 44).

## Natural methods

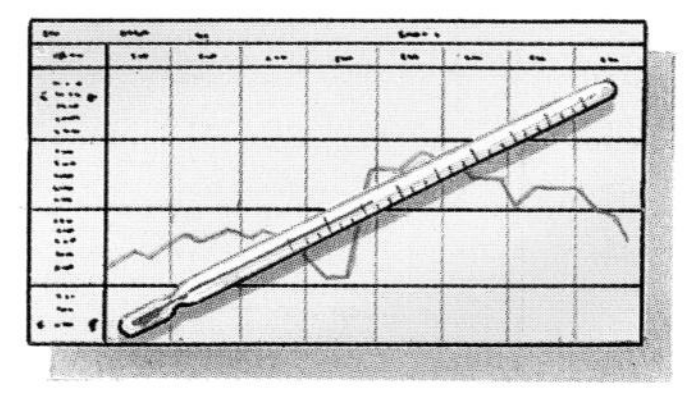

**Temperature graph**

An ovum lives for only about 24 hours after ovulation. Sperm can live inside a woman's body for up to five days. This means that if a couple do not have intercourse from five days before ovulation to one day after, in theory conception should not take place. However, the trouble with natural methods of contraception is that it is extremely difficult to predict ovulation.

Couples try to figure it out from the dates of the woman's last period; by noting fluctuations in her temperature during her cycle; and by examining a fluid produced by the cervix for changes in its appearance. Even using all three methods together, the failure rate is high. With the help of a specially trained teacher, there is more chance of success. It is also possible to buy kits which monitor ovulation more accurately by measuring hormone levels. These are expensive.

## Injections and implants

**Injection**

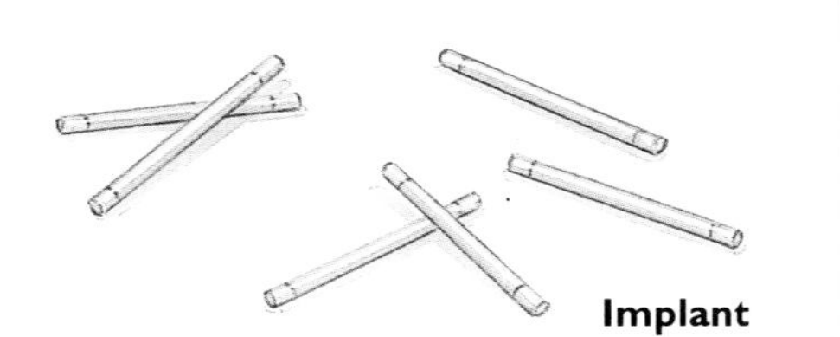

**Implant**

These are effective, long term methods of contraception. An injection releases progestogen into the woman's body and this prevents ovulation. One injection lasts for two or three months.

Implants are small, soft tubes which are inserted by a doctor or nurse under the skin of a woman's upper arm. They gradually release progestogen into her body to prevent an egg and a sperm meeting. An implant is effective for up to five years and the woman has regular checkups during this time. The implant can be removed if necessary.

Side effects of both injections and implants can include changes in the woman's periods and weight gain.

## Non-methods of contraception

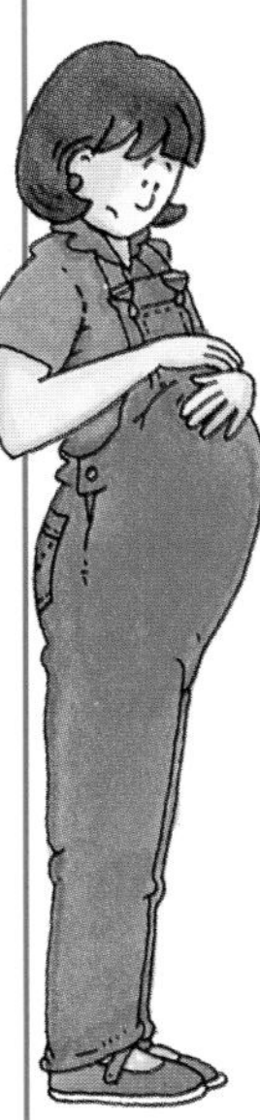

Here are a few myths about contraception. "The woman cannot become pregnant if ...
1...the man withdraws his penis from the vagina before he ejaculates." This is untrue because sperm leak out of the penis before ejaculation. If the man ejaculates near the vagina after withdrawal, sperm may still get into it.
2...she lies on top of the man during intercourse or if the couple both stand up." Gravity may mean that fewer sperm swim up into the uterus but very many still will.
3...she is having a period." Sperm can swim through menstrual blood and there may be an ovum in one of the ducts even though it is early in the woman's cycle.
4...she goes to the bathroom immediately after intercourse." The sperm will not be flushed out of her body because the vagina and urethra are totally separate.
5...it is the first time she has had intercourse or she has only just started having periods." It is true that some girls start having periods before they are ovulating properly but, as a rule, anyone who has started her periods, or is about to have her first period, may become pregnant.
6...she does not have an orgasm." Contractions of the uterus during orgasm may help to suck the sperm in but they also enter very easily without them.

## Failure rate

You can see how reliable different methods of contraception are below. The figure given shows how many women in a hundred get pregnant using that method for a year.

| | |
|---|---|
| **Combined pill** | **almost 0%** |
| **Progestogen-only pill** | **1%** |
| **IUD** | **1-2%** |
| **IUS** | **almost 0%** |
| **Diaphragm and cap** | **4-8%** |
| **Male condom** | **2%** |
| **Female condom** | **5%** |
| **Injections** | **almost 0%** |
| **Implant** | **2%** |
| **Natural methods** | **5-15%** |
| **No contraception** | **80-90%** |

## Emergency contraception

If a couple forgets to use contraception or something goes wrong with it, for example a condom splits, there are two methods of emergency contraception. These can be provided only by a doctor.

One is for the woman to take two doses of special pills; if this method is started within three days (72 hours) after intercourse, it will usually prevent ovulation, or stop a fertilized ovum from embedding itself in the uterus. Emergency pills cannot be taken regularly.

The other method is for the woman to have an IUD inserted (see page 31) within five days after intercourse.

## Abortion

This is not a method of contraception but an operation to end a pregnancy once it has begun. The contents of the woman's uterus are sucked or scraped out or, if pregnancy is fairly advanced, she is given drugs which bring on labor (the birth process). The risks of the operation include infection.

In many countries abortion is illegal. In others it is legal only under certain conditions. In the US, the laws regulating abortion vary from state to state, but in general, the more advanced a pregnancy is, the more restricted are the circumstances in which an abortion may be performed.

# Food

A healthy diet is important no matter how old you are, but it is especially necessary at puberty, when you are growing and developing very fast. Food, combined with oxygen in the air you breathe, is a fuel which helps you to grow and gives you energy. Different types of food do different jobs in your body so you need to eat a good balance of all the types. Water, too, is essential.

## Protein

Over ten percent of the human body is made of a substance called protein, so you need to eat protein to grow and for your body to repair itself. For this reason, protein is especially important at puberty. Good sources are lean meat, fish, cheese, eggs, milk, nuts and beans.

## Carbohydrates

These provide most of your energy. There are two forms: starches and sugars. It is better to eat starchy foods, such as bread, potatoes, rice and pasta, rather than sweet foods such as cake, cookies, chocolate and ice cream or sweetened drinks. Sugar has no benefits apart from giving you energy and it is very bad for your teeth.

## Fats

These also give you energy. There are two types of fat: "saturated", which is found in animal products such as meat, butter, lard, cream and most margarines, and "polyunsaturated", which is found in non-animal products such as liquid vegetable oils, certain margarines and nuts. Experts think that eating too much saturated fat may contribute to heart disease.

## Vitamins and minerals

You need small amounts of about 15 different vitamins and 20 minerals for essential chemical processes to take place in your body. The vitamins and minerals are found in a wide range of foods. If you are eating a balanced diet and are healthy, it is not usually necessary to take vitamin and mineral supplements.

Calcium is a mineral. It is found in foods such as milk and cheese and is important at puberty because it makes your bones and teeth strong. Salt is also an essential mineral, though people in developed countries usually eat more of it than is necessary and this may play a part in heart disease.

## Fiber

This is not really a food. It consists of a type of carbohydrate that you cannot digest. This travels through your digestive tract in bulk, making the muscles of your intestines work efficiently, preventing constipation. Fiber may also help prevent serious diseases of the intestines such as cancer. It is found in vegetables, fruit, whole wheat bread and pasta, wholegrain cereals, brown rice, pulses, beans and nuts.

## Food groups

Dietitians divide food into the four groups shown below. You should eat about four servings from each of groups 2 and 4 every day, and about two servings from each of groups 1 and 3.

1. Lean meat, fish, eggs, lentils, beans and nuts.

2. Bread, potatoes, cereals, rice and pasta (preferably wholegrain varieties).

3. Milk, cheese and yogurt.

4. Fruit and vegetables.

## Weight

Your weight increases even more spectacularly than your height at puberty, as a result of your larger bones and internal organs, and more muscle and fat. The female sex hormones make females gain more fat than males. This is an energy storage they can draw on during pregnancy. It is not easy to suggest ideal weights, as people are such different builds.

**Age 10**

**55% of final weight**

**59% of final weight**

## Calories

**About 40 calories**

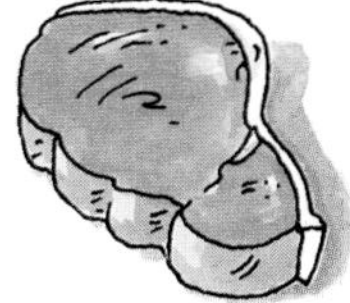

**About 340 calories**

The amount of energy that can be produced from food is measured in calories. Different foods have different numbers of calories. How many calories people need depends on how much energy they use up. Going through puberty takes such a lot of energy that you need as many calories then as a full-grown adult does. Males generally use more energy than females because they are bigger.

**Male at puberty 2,900 calories a day approx.**

**Female at puberty 2,150 calories a day approx.**

## Being too fat

Any calories which are not converted into energy are stored as fat under your skin. On average, fat people die younger and suffer more from certain illnesses, including heart disease, than thin people. If you think you may be too fat, ask a doctor or a dietitian. If you weigh over 13kg (29lb) more than the average weight of all your friends, you may well be eating too many fattening foods. The best way to lose some weight is to cut down on fatty foods, especially fried foods such as chips, and sugary foods and drinks. Some foods, for example milk shakes, ice cream and cookies are mostly fat and sugar. Fiber will fill you up without giving you calories. Don't be tempted onto a crash diet. These are unbalanced and you will put back any weight you lose once you stop the diet.

## Anorexia

This serious illness mainly affects girls at puberty. They become obsessed with losing weight, thinking they are fat when they are not. An anorexic loses weight dramatically, stops having periods and denies that anything is wrong. The cause may be psychological - perhaps the girl does not want to grow up and tries to keep her childlike shape by starving herself.

# Exercise

Exercise is an important part of good health. By making sure you get plenty of exercise during puberty, you help your body to develop as fully as possible. Exercise makes not only the muscles of your skeleton strong but also your heart, which is a muscle too, your lungs and your bones. The younger you are when you first start getting fit, the easier you will find it and the more likely you are to avoid certain illnesses, especially heart and circulatory disease, as you get older.

## What can exercise do?

Exercise can have many benefits. Here are some of them.

1. Exercise makes you strong by increasing the size and strength of your muscles. Without it, muscles waste and turn to fat.

2. It keeps your joints supple so they do not stiffen up and cause aches and pains.

3. It makes you breathe deeper and take in more oxygen. The food you eat must be combined with oxygen inside your body before it can give you energy.

4. It strengthens your heart so that it pumps blood more efficiently. This means it can do more work with less effort. Just running for a bus can strain an unfit person's heart.

5. It improves your circulation by making your blood vessels more elastic and opening up new channels. This means that food and oxygen, which are carried in your blood, get around your body more efficiently.

6. It improves your speed of reaction, coordination and grace by making your brain and nervous system work more efficiently.

7. It helps to keep you slim by using up calories.

8. It helps you relax and overcome stress, which can cause illness. You feel generally healthier.

## What exercise to choose?

Almost any type of exercise is better than none, but for general health and fitness it is best to do a sport which has as many of the benefits shown on the left as possible. These include swimming, soccer, aerobics, energetic dancing and cycling. The best types of exercise of all are thought to be swimming and fast walking.

## Posture

Good posture is difficult to learn but it is well worth the effort. Once you know how to stand or sit correctly, it is actually less tiring than slumping, as it places less strain on your body.

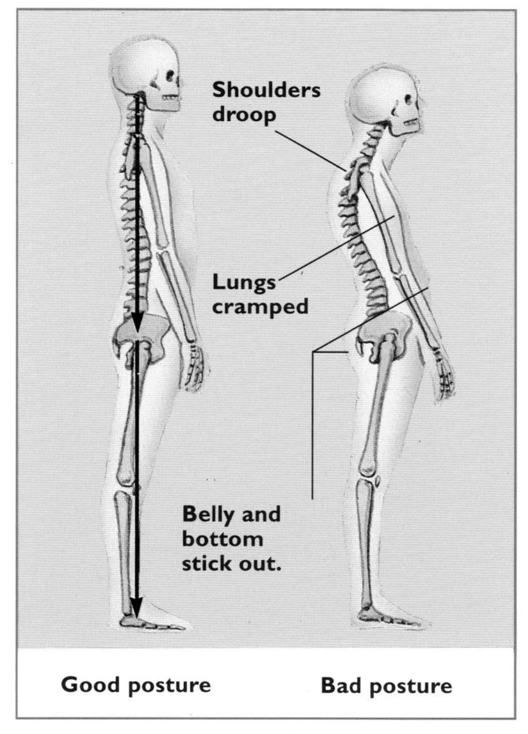


Try to imagine a vertical line running through your pelvis from just behind your ear to just in front of your ankle, as shown in the diagram on the left. The one on the right shows the strain put on your body by standing incorrectly.

## Sleep

You will probably find you need quite a lot of sleep at puberty because you are growing fast and using up so much energy. Most 10-14 year-olds need about ten hours sleep a night and 14-18 year-olds about nine hours but it can vary. The best guide to how much sleep you need is the way you feel.

The reason for sleep is not really understood. During sleep, your muscles relax and your heart and breathing rates fall, so it may be a period of recovery and repair for the body. Dreaming may be a way of making sense of things that have happened to you, and part of learning.

## Rest

Rest can be physical relaxation such as sleep, or just a change of activity. After exercising hard, sitting and reading a book or watching television will rest your muscles and heart. After studying hard, doing some kind of exercise will rest your brain.

## Shoes

Your feet are not fully formed until you are about 20, so it is important to wear well-fitting shoes all the way through puberty. If your shoes are too short, your feet will not grow correctly; if they are too narrow or pointed, you may get corns or painful bunions; if they are not flexible, your muscles will not develop right. High heels alter the natural distribution of your weight, causing strain to your feet and to your body as a whole.

# Smoking, drinking and other drugs

Drugs affect the way people think, feel and behave. They can be habit-forming, so the person using them becomes dependent on them mentally; or they can be addictive, which means that their body gets used to having them and is disturbed without them. Both alcohol and the nicotine in tobacco are addictive.

Many drugs can cause serious illness. For instance, one in every three cases of cancer is thought to be directly related to cigarette smoking. Many people ignore the health hazards and continue to smoke and drink heavily, or take other drugs; some of them will try to encourage you to do the same.

## Smoking

1

It is estimated that every cigarette shortens the smoker's life by 14 minutes. Most heavy smokers die of diseases caused by smoking. Nonsmokers are at risk, too, just by being in a smoky atmosphere. It is always worth giving up smoking. Unless disease has already set in, the risks gradually decrease until, ten years after giving up, they almost disappear.

Two of the most poisonous chemicals in tobacco smoke are tar and nicotine.

2

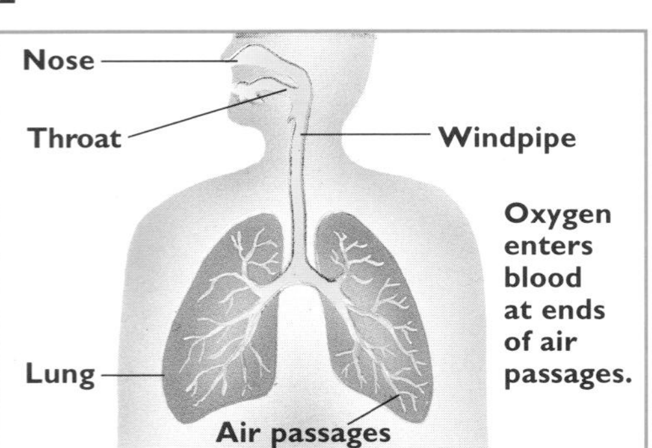


The air you breathe has to be cleaned before it reaches the lowest part of your lungs. This is the purpose of the slippery liquid called mucus which you have in your nose and upper air passages. The mucus traps dirt and bacteria, while tiny hairs called cilia waft the mucus away from your lungs toward your nose and throat.

3

The tar in tobacco smoke irritates the air passages, making them narrower, increasing mucus production and making the cilia less efficient, so that the mucus, dirt and bacteria stay in the lungs. This causes "smoker's cough", which is really a symptom of bronchitis (inflammation of the air passages) and makes the lungs more prone to infection.

4

Nine out of ten cases of lung cancer occur in smokers and tar is thought to be responsible.

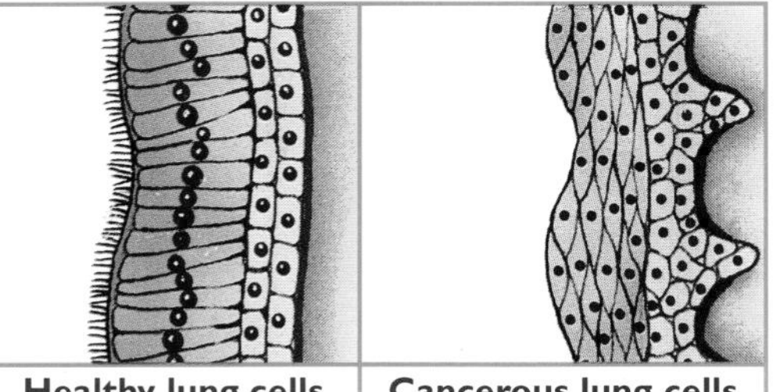


5

Nicotine acts on the brain and nervous system and may be the substance which gives some smokers pleasure. It also makes people unused to smoking feel faint and sick. Nicotine makes the heart beat faster and narrows the blood vessels, contributing to heart and circulatory disease.

## Alcohol

Alcohol is a depressant drug, which means that it slows down all the body processes. Small doses make people feel relaxed and confident. Larger doses slow your reactions and affect judgement and coordination, which is why it is very dangerous to drink and drive. The drinker may become sick and dizzy, or even fall unconscious, adding the danger of choking on vomit.

**Spirits: 40% alcohol approx.** **Wine: 12% alcohol approx.** **Beer: 5% alcohol approx.**

These effects depend partly on how concentrated the alcohol is in the drink. Spirits, such as whisky or vodka, are the strongest, then wine, then beer. The person's size and how used they are to alcohol also count. Large people are usually more resistant to alcohol than small ones.

The long term effects of heavy drinking include getting fat, as alcohol contains calories, though no nourishment; inflammation of the stomach leading to ulcers; shriveling and scarring of the liver (cirrhosis), and damage to the brain, kidneys and muscles, including the heart.

The brain of a person who regularly drinks heavily struggles constantly against the depressant effect of the alcohol to keep them awake. If they then stop drinking, their brain continues compensating, which makes the person excited, nervous, shaky and fidgety until they get another drink. This is an example of addiction.

## Illegal drugs

There are lots of drugs that are illegal to use or sell. Ecstasy and cannabis, for example, are both illegal drugs.

Different drugs are taken in different ways: swallowed, sniffed, smoked or injected, and they have different effects. No one can ever be sure how a drug will affect them. The same drug can have a different effect on different people, and even on the same person at different times. It is impossible to know how strong a drug is or exactly what is in it, as the drug itself is often mixed with other substances. The large number of slang names for different drugs can be confusing and the names are changing all the time.

Drugs can be habit-forming or addictive, so that once someone starts using them, it is very hard to stop. They can be extremely harmful and even lead to death. The best way to avoid problems with drugs is simply not to take them.

## Solvents

Inhaling the chemicals in aerosol sprays, cigarette lighter fuel or solvent-based glues has a similar effect on the nervous system to alcohol but is much more dangerous. Some people suffer long term damage and there have been many cases of sudden death after sniffing. Sniffing from a plastic bag or spraying the substances directly into the mouth can cause death by suffocation.

## Other drugs

Even pills, tablets, powders and other drugs which you can buy from pharmacies or drugstores without a prescription, such as aspirins and cold remedies, can damage your health or kill you, if you take too many or take them too often. They are all chemicals which are not natural to your body. If you have a headache, ask yourself if you really need an aspirin or if lying down quietly and relaxing might work just as well. You should never take any drug which has been prescribed for someone else.

# Keeping clean

Keeping clean becomes more important at puberty than it was during childhood. This is because your skin starts producing more of the kind of substances which can cause unpleasant smells or even bad health if you forget to wash them off regularly.

## Skin

This picture shows a slice through your skin so you can see what it is like below the surface.

Surface skin: your surface skin is called the epidermis. Its top layer is dead and is constantly being worn away as you come into contact with things. It is then replaced by skin from a layer lower down in the epidermis.

Sebaceous glands: these produce an oily substance called sebum, which coats your hair and skin, helping to keep them waterproof and supple. At puberty, the glands start producing more sebum and this can cause greasy hair and pimples.

Sweat glands: even when you are not hot, sweat is constantly coming up to the surface of your skin from your sweat glands and coming out through your pores. The sweat helps to rid your body of waste and keep your temperature stable. At puberty, you start to sweat more.



## Washing

You need to wash every day to get rid of dirt, dead skin, sebum and sweat.

Your sweat glands are most numerous under your arms and around your genitals, so it is particularly important to wash these parts of your body every day.

## Armpits

Many people find that the numerous sweat glands under their arms make them sweat a lot, especially if they are excited or nervous. Using an underarm deodorant or antiperspirant helps to stop smells from developing before you have a chance to wash. Deodorants work by slowing down the growth of bacteria on the sweat, and antiperspirants make you sweat less by closing some of your pores.

## Teeth

Most people have all their adult teeth by about age 16, except for the four wisdom teeth, which come through later. To guard against tooth and gum disease, you should brush your teeth at least twice a day.

Tooth decay is caused by bacteria which feed on sugar in your mouth. They multiply and form a substance called plaque. This contains acids, which eat holes into the tooth. If these are not filled, the tooth eventually starts to ache, and an infection or abscess may develop. The tooth may become loose if the gum is damaged.

It is therefore important to go to the dentist regularly. You can help by eating and drinking less sugar and by using fluoride toothpaste, which strengthens your teeth.

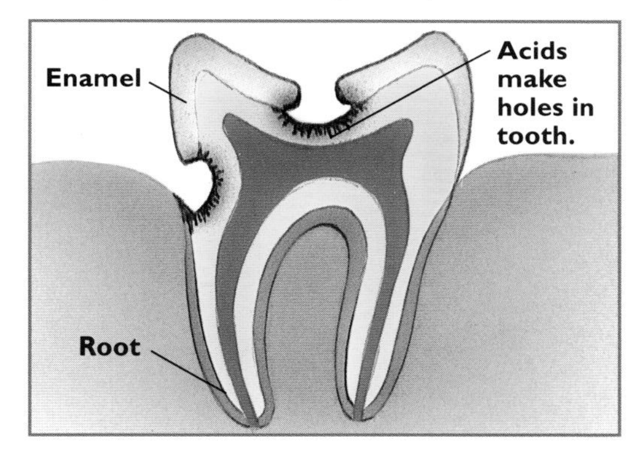


## Genitals

Urine, vaginal fluids, menstrual blood, semen and smegma are all clean, though once they leave the body, bacteria can breed on them as well as on the sweat produced in the area. Bacteria can enter the body through the vagina, urethral opening or penis, so you need to wash the genital area every day.

The rectum contains many bacteria, so it is important, especially for females, to wash and dry from front to back, to avoid spreading them to the nearby vagina or urethra. Males need to roll back their foreskin and wash gently underneath.

Wash with mild soap and warm water. Don't use deodorant or antiperspirant in this area, as they can cause irritation or infection. After washing, remember to put on clean underwear.

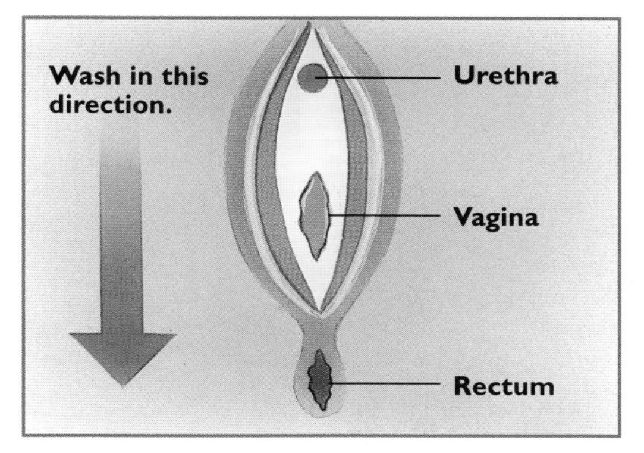


## How to clean your teeth

It is important to clean your teeth thoroughly rather than vigorously. Hold the brush at a slight angle and brush up and down, not across, with small strokes, so that the bristles get between your teeth. Work your way right around your mouth and brush the backs of your teeth as well as the fronts. You should also floss your teeth once a day with dental floss.

It is unhygienic to use anyone else's toothbrush (see also page 44).

**Brush up and down, not from side to side.**

## Discharges

A certain amount of vaginal discharge is normal in females. The vagina's lubricating fluid leaks out and so does the fluid produced by the cervix during the menstrual cycle. These fluids vary from clear to milky in appearance and have almost no smell. Some girls have a whitish discharge for a few months before their periods start.

If your normal discharge becomes a lot heavier or thicker, changes color, or starts to smell, itch or burn, it probably means that bacteria which normally live harmlessly in the vagina have gotten out of hand and you have an infection. The doctor can treat it with suppositories or antibiotics. Males should go to the doctor if they have any discharge at all from the penis.

## Face

Many experts say that soap is bad for your face because it is a detergent and can dry up sebum too much. On the other hand, people at puberty tend to have an excess of sebum anyway and you may find that the cleansing creams and lotions you can buy give you pimples, as well as being expensive. The best thing to do is figure out what suits your skin.

## Pimples

It is thought that changes in hormone levels during puberty make your sebaceous glands produce an excess of sebum. Your sebaceous glands are most numerous on your face and back. Testosterone is probably the hormone most involved, so pimples, or acne, are more common in males than females.

If the sebum accumulates at the opening of a sebaceous gland, you get a blackhead. If it builds up below the surface, you get a whitehead or a reddish lump. The pimple may be infected by bacteria.

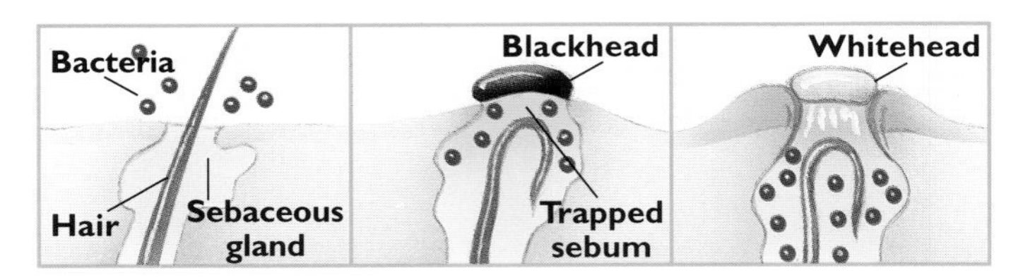


If you are prone to pimples, try washing your face frequently using mild, unperfumed or antiseptic soap and warm water. Some people find that cutting out certain foods, such as colas or chocolate, improves their skin. Males can try wiping their razor with liquid antiseptic after shaving. Trying to camouflage pimples with greasy makeup will only make them worse. If you have a real problem with your skin, do go to the doctor.

You should not really squeeze pimples, because of the risk of damaging the skin and spreading any infection. If you do squeeze them, make sure your hands are completely clean and only squeeze blackheads.

## Hair

Your hair needs to be washed to clear it of dirt, dead cells, sebum and sweat. The amount of sebum you produce determines whether you have dry or greasy hair. Greasy hair may need to be washed once a day; once a week may be enough for dry hair.

Dandruff consists of dead cells from the head. It is more likely to affect people with dry hair. It is rarely infectious and using a "medicated" shampoo is unlikely to help. If it gets very bad, go to the doctor.

## Nails

**Correct way to cut your big toenail.**

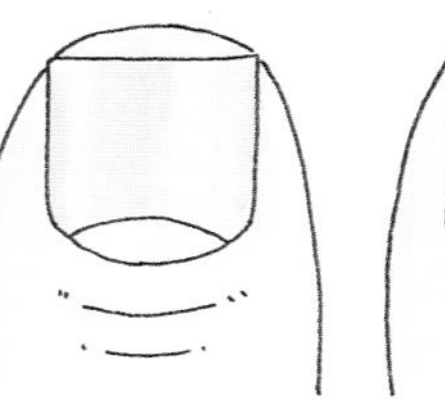

**Wrong way to cut your big toenail.**

Keep your nails clean by scrubbing underneath with a nail brush.

You can cut your finger nails using scissors or nail clippers, or file them with an emery board. Metal files tend to split the nails. If your nails break easily, keep them short.

For your toenails, you need very sharp scissors. Cut the nails straight across. Shaping them can make the edges of the nail grow into the flesh and, if they actually break the skin, cause an infection. This is an ingrown toenail.

# Growing up and your feelings

As you become physically and emotionally more mature, you become more independent and your relationships with the people around you also alter. Some people find these changes stressful at times.

It may help to remember that other people are experiencing the same thing, and that older people went through similar experiences at one time. The way you feel may also be affected by physical changes in your body, over which you have no control.

## Independence

As you grow up, you will probably want to take more responsibility for your own life and actions. This can sometimes cause conflict with your parents, who have to adjust to the idea that you are becoming more independent.

## Identity

Thinking about what kind of person you are and about what you want to do and be in the future is an important part of growing up. It can feel lonely and confusing sometimes, coming to terms with your adult personality.

## Friends

Most teenagers make close friends and some even fall in love. You may form a close group of friends but beware of feeling that you must always do what the rest of the group do, especially if you feel uncomfortable or unhappy about it.

## Moods

At times, you may feel moody and irritable without really knowing why. Changes in your body's hormone levels can be partly to blame for this. Things usually improve as you get used to your adult body and feelings.

## Shyness

Many adolescents suffer from shyness. They lack confidence in their looks and personality. How much you suffer and how you cope depends on your individual character. Remember that others often feel shy even if they do not look it.

# AIDS

## What is AIDS?

AIDS stands for acquired immune deficiency syndrome. It is a condition in which a person's immune system, which defends the body against disease, breaks down. This means that the person is likely to get illnesses which they would normally fight off easily. These illnesses can be fatal.

## What causes AIDS?

AIDS is caused by a virus called HIV (human immunodeficiency virus). No one really knows where the virus first came from. A large number of people who have the virus in Western countries are homosexual men but other people can get it too. In Africa, men and women are affected equally. Most people who are infected with HIV eventually go on to develop AIDS but this may not be for several years.

## What does HIV do?

When someone catches any virus, certain white blood cells in their body produce antibodies which attack and kill the virus. HIV can actually destroy these white blood cells so that the person is unable to fight off infections.

## How is the virus passed on?

HIV lives in body fluids such as semen, vaginal fluid and blood. There are two main ways in which it is passed on from one person to another. One is when semen or vaginal fluid from an infected person enters another person's body during sexual activity.

The other is when an infected person's blood gets into another person's body. For this reason, drug users who inject using shared equipment are at risk.

Women with the virus can pass it on to their baby during pregnancy, at birth or in breast milk.

## Medical research and AIDS?

There is so far no cure for AIDS, although a lot is known about HIV. Doctors can find out whether someone has the virus by testing their blood to see if it contains anti-HIV antibodies. If it does, the person is said to be "HIV positive".

A great deal of research is being done to try to produce more effective drugs for treating people with HIV and AIDS, and to develop a vaccine so that people could be immunized against it.

## Preventing the spread of HIV

The fewer sexual partners a person has, the less risk they have of coming into contact with someone who has the virus. If a person's partner is infected, having vaginal or anal intercourse, or oral sex (see the glossary) is risky. Using a condom during intercourse helps to reduce the risk.

Because of the risk of getting infected blood in the bloodstream, anything which punctures the skin is risky unless it has been properly sterilized. This includes ear-piercing equipment, as well as tattooing and acupuncture needles.

Drug users who inject drugs should never share equipment.

It is unwise to share razors or toothbrushes (because many people's gums bleed when they brush their teeth).

## Ways in which HIV is not passed on

HIV only survives for a short time outside the body, so it is not passed on by ordinary everyday contact. You cannot catch the virus by touching an infected person or objects used by an infected person, such as towels or toilet seats. There is no known case of anyone catching the virus from saliva, for example by kissing or using the same dishes, or from tears or sweat, although these are all body fluids. It seems that, although the virus can live in these fluids, it cannot be passed on through them. Swimming pools are safe because the chemicals in the water kill the virus.

In many countries, including the US, needles and syringes used by doctors, nurses, dentists and other medical staff are always sterilized between patients, a new needle is used for each donor of blood to the blood transfusion service and all blood is tested for HIV before being given to anyone needing a transfusion.

# Glossary

Here are some words you may hear whose meanings you do not know. If the word you want is not listed below, try looking in the index at the back of this book, as it may be explained elsewhere.

*Acne*. The condition of having lots of pimples, usually on the face, upper chest, back and shoulders. It is a combination of inflamed and pus-containing pimples and blackheads, probably caused by hormone activity.

*Adultery*. Sexual intercourse between a person who is married and someone who is not their husband or wife.

*Amenorrhea*. Absence of periods.

*Anal intercourse*. Intercourse in which the penis enters the rectum (back passage).

*Androgynous*. Looking partly male and partly female in appearance.

*Aphrodisiac*. A substance which increases sexual desire.

*Birth control*. Contraception (see right).

*BO*. Body odor, caused by not washing often enough, or not using deodorant.

*Brothel*. House where prostitutes have sex with their clients.

*Bulimia*. Illness in which the sufferer, usually female, eats vast amounts of fattening food at one sitting and then, to avoid putting on weight, makes herself vomit. Related to anorexia.

*Calendar method*. Unreliable method of contraception which involves predicting a "safe period" for intercourse from the dates of the woman's periods.

*Castration*. Removal of a male's testicles.

*Celibacy*. Not having sexual intercourse for a longish period of time.

*Cells*. The basic living units of which the body is composed.

*Cervix*. The lower end of the uterus, which opens to let the baby through during birth.

*Chastity*. Virginity (see page 47) or celibacy.

*Child abuse*. Mistreating a child, that is anyone under 18, including forcing or persuading her/him into sexual activity. In many countries, including the US, this is illegal and there are organizations which help children who are being mistreated (see page 48).

*Clap*. Slang word for gonorrhea (see page 46).

*Coitus*. Sexual intercourse.

*Coitus interruptus*. The withdrawal method of contraception (see page 47).

*Conceive*. Become pregnant.

*Conception*. The joining of a sperm cell and an egg cell. This is the start of a new individual.

*Contraception*. Prevention of sexual intercourse from leading to pregnancy.

*Copulation*. Sexual intercourse.

*Crabs*. Pubic lice (see page 47).

*Cystitis*. Inflammation of the bladder, which causes pain when going to the bathroom. Cystitis is usually caused by bacterial infection and is more common in females than males.

*Delivery*. Labor; birth.

*Embryo*. A developing baby in the early stages of pregnancy.

*Erotic*. To do with sexual love; producing sexual desire.

*Family planning*. Contraception; birth control.

*Feminist*. Someone who wants to improve the rights of women.

*Fertilization*. Conception (see above).

*Fetus.* A developing baby between the 12th week and the end of pregnancy.

*Flasher.* Someone who displays their genitals in public.

*French letter.* Slang expression for condom.

*Gland.* A group of cells which produces and releases substances which have an effect on another part of the body.

*Gonorrhea.* One of the most common sexually transmitted diseases. It can usually be cured by antibiotics.

*Gynecologist.* Doctor who specializes in diseases of the female reproductive system.

*Herpes (genital).* Also called herpes type 2. A sexually transmitted disease for which no cure is yet known. There is no connection between genital herpes and herpes simplex (herpes type 1), which is a cold sore.

*Hormones.* Chemical substances which control certain processes in the body. They are produced in glands and are carried around the body in the blood.

*Hysterectomy.* Operation to remove a woman's uterus.

*Implantation.* The embedding of a fertilized egg in the lining of the uterus.

*Impotence.* Inability of a male to get an erection or have an orgasm.

*Incest.* Sexual intercourse between two people who are too closely related to be allowed to be legally married, e.g. brother and sister, father and daughter.

*Infertility.* Inability to have children.

*Labor.* The process by which a baby leaves its mother's body; birth.

*Libido.* Sex drive.

*Making out.* . Sexual contact which involves kissing and touching the partner's body but does not include intercourse.



*Male chauvinist pig.* A sexist male who treats females as though they are inferior to males and should not have the same rights.

*Masochist.* Someone who gets pleasure from having pain inflicted on them.

*Missionary position.* A position for sexual intercourse with the couple lying facing each other, the man on top.

*Molest.* To make unwanted sexual advances to someone.

*NSU (Non-specific urethritis).* Inflammation of the urethra - the tube leading from the bladder to the outside of the body. This is a sexually transmitted disease which affects males only.

*Nymphomaniac.* Woman with uncontrollable sexual desire.

*Oral sex.* Stimulation of the genitals by mouth.

*Ovary.* Female sex gland which produces eggs. Each female has a pair of ovaries.

*Ovulation.* The release of an ovum from an ovary. In most women this happens about once a month.

*Ovum (ova).* Egg cell (cells).

*Pedophile.* Adult who is sexually attracted to children.

*Perversion.* Abnormal sexual activity.

*Petting.* Making out.

*Phallus.* Image of an erect penis. If something is described as phallic, it resembles an erect penis.

*Placenta.* The organ which transfers food and oxygen from the mother to the baby in the uterus, and transfers the baby's waste products back to the mother.

*Platonic (friendship).* Nonsexual.

*Pornography.* Pictures or writing aimed at producing sexual arousal.

*Pox.* Slang word for syphilis (see below).

*Premature ejaculation.* Male orgasm and ejaculation reached too quickly.

*Promiscuity.* Sexual intercourse with several different casual acquaintances over a short period of time.

*Prostitute.* Person who has sex with someone in return for payment.

*Pubic lice.* A sexually transmitted disease caused by a blood-sucker called the crab louse which lives in pubic hair.

*Rape.* Forcing someone to have sexual intercourse, either vaginal or anal, against their will.

*Reproduction.* Production of offspring.

*Sadist.* Someone who gets pleasure from inflicting pain.

*Sexist.* Someone who thinks that people should behave in a certain way because of their sex.

*Sexual harassment.* Making of unwanted sexual advances to someone; molesting.

*Sixty-nine.* Simultaneous oral stimulation of the genitals, so-called because of the position of the couple's bodies. Also referred to in French as *soixante-neuf.*

*Sodomy.* Anal intercourse between two males.

*Solicit.* To approach people in public places offering sex in return for payment.

*Sterilization.* A surgical operation to make someone permanently incapable of having children. Generally, people only have a sterilization if they already have children and are certain they do not want any more. Male sterilization is easier to do than female because the male sex organs are outside the body.

*Syphilis.* A serious sexually transmitted disease, now rare, which can be cured by antibiotics.

*Temperature method.* Unreliable method of contraception which involves predicting a "safe period" for intercourse from changes in the woman's temperature during her menstrual cycle.

*Testes.* Testicles.

*Transsexual.* Someone who wants to change sex or who has already had a sex change operation.

*Transvestite.* Someone who wears clothes of the opposite sex.

*Umbilical cord.* The cord which connects the baby and the placenta in the uterus.

*Uterus.* The stretchy bag inside a female, in which a baby grows during pregnancy.

*Vagina.* The tube which leads from the outside of a female's body to her uterus.

*Vasectomy.* Male sterilization.

*Virgin.* Someone who has never had sexual intercourse.

*Voyeur.* Someone who gets sexual pleasure from secretly watching other people's sexual activities or from secretly watching people undressing; a peeping tom.

*Whore.* Prostitute.

*Withdrawal method.* An extremely unreliable method of contraception in which the man withdraws his penis from the vagina before he ejaculates.

*Womb.* Uterus (see above).

*Yeast infection (candidiasis).* A common sexually transmitted disease which can develop without sexual contact. It is caused by a yeast fungus. Symptoms occur mainly in women and include increased vaginal discharge, itching, or pain when going to the bathroom. Treatment is with anti-fungal suppositories or pills, and sometimes cream for the male partner.

## Useful contacts

If you have a problem and you feel you cannot get help or advice from anyone you know, one of the organizations below may be able to help you. Calls made to numbers starting with 1-800 are free; all others are charged at regular long distance rates.

For general information on sex and pregnancy:
SIECUS, 130 W. 42nd Street, Suite 350, New York, NY 10036-7802
1-212-819-9770

For sex and pregnancy information or services:
Planned Parenthood 1-800-230-PLAN
(will connect you to the nearest clinic)

For advice about sexually transmitted diseases:
STD Hotline 1-800-227-8922

For advice about AIDS:
AIDS teen hotline 1-800-440-TEEN
AIDS Information Clearing House
1-800-458-5231

For information about homosexuality:
Gay and Lesbian National Hotline
1-888-843-4564

For information about bisexuality:
BiNet USA 301-986-7186

For advice about drug problems:
National Institute on Drug Abuse
1-800-662-HELP

For problems related to alcohol:
Alcoholics Anonymous National Office
1-212-870-3400
Al-Anon 1-800-356-9996 (for free literature packet) 1-800-344-2666 (for meeting information)

For advice about smoking:
American Cancer Society 1-800-227-2345

For advice about eating disorders:
Anorexia/Bulimia Hotline 1-800-762-3334
Bulimia Anorexia Self Help 1-800-227-4785

For advice about child abuse:
National Child Abuse Hotline/Department of Social Services 1-800-342-3720
Childhelp National Child Abuse Hotline/ Voices for Children
1-800-4ACHILD (422-4453)
The police

For legal advice:
Look in your telephone book for legal aid organizations.

Feeling desperate:
Teen Hotline 1-800-234-TEEN
National Youth Crisis Hotline 1-800-442-HOPE
National Runaway Hotline 1-800-621-4000

USBORNE FACTS OF LIFE

# Part 2

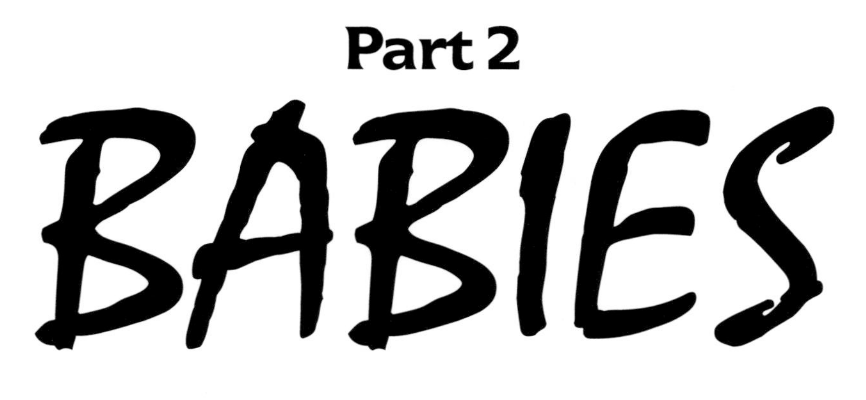


**Robyn Gee**

**Designed by Roger Priddy**

**Revision by Susan Meredith, Isaac Quaye and Susannah Owen**

**Illustrated by Sue Stitt,
David Gifford, Kuo Kang Chen and Lee Montgomery**

**Consultants: Judy Cunnington, Relate Marriage Guidance Council;
Fran Reader, Senior Registrar in Obstetrics and Gynaecology,
University College Hospital, London;
Judith Schott, SRN, Antenatal teacher trained by the National Childbirth Trust;
Dr Peter Hope, Research Registrar, Neonatal Unit,
University College Hospital, London.**

# Contents - part 2

# About part 2

This part of the book tells the fascinating story of how each new person arrives in the world. It describes how babies start and what happens to both a mother and her baby during pregnancy. It explains exactly what happens when a baby is born and gives you some idea of how a new baby may feel, look and behave. There is lots of information on how to help look after a baby, including some useful safety tips in the Babysitter's guide at the end of the book.

The key stages in a baby's development, up to the age of around two, are also included. This section may be of particular interest if someone you know is expecting a baby, or if you are thinking about a career which involves some aspect of pregnancy or childcare. If you want to find out more information than is included here, look at the Useful contacts section on page 48 for a list of organizations to get in touch with.

Most of the difficult words relating to pregnancy and birth are explained when they first appear, but if you come across any words that you do not understand, or you forget what they mean, try looking them up in the Glossary on pages 45-47.

The colors used in the pictures of things inside the body are not true to life. Most of these things are also shown either much larger or much smaller than life-size but, where possible, an indication of the actual size has been given.

To avoid constantly repeating "the baby" or writing "he or she", we have used "he" in some places and "she" in others. When referring to an unborn baby, however, we have used "it", as people usually do this when they are talking.

From the moment a baby starts, even before it is the size of one of the commas on this page, it is a unique individual. When people talk about how babies grow and develop, they tend to talk about averages - the average weight and height at a particular age, the average time they spend sleeping, the average age at which they learn to do things. Perfectly normal babies, however, vary from these averages enormously and very few babies are average in all respects. Where averages are given, they are merely a guideline about what to expect if you know very little about babies.

# How a baby starts

Each human being is made up of billions and billions of separate living units called cells. The story of how a new human being comes into existence begins with just two of these tiny cells - an egg cell and a sperm cell. Egg cells are produced inside the mother's body and sperm in the father's. A baby starts when an egg cell and a sperm meet and join together to form one new cell. The moment when the egg and sperm join is called conception or fertilization.

## Egg cells

**1** An egg cell is also called an ovum. (The plural of ovum is ova.) When a baby girl is born, she already has about 400,000 ova stored inside her body in two ovaries. When she grows up, an ovum ripens each month in one of her ovaries and is released. This is called ovulation.

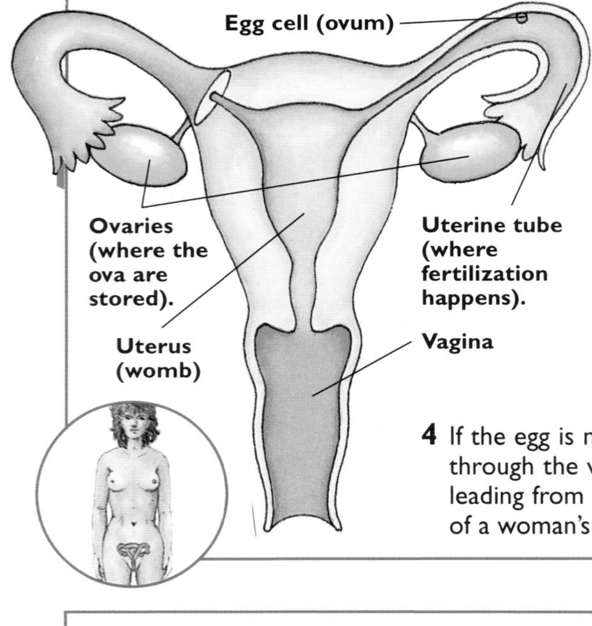


**2**

The ovum is released from the ovary into a tube called a uterine or Fallopian tube. If it meets a sperm while it is in the tube, it may be joined, or fertilized, by the sperm.

**3**

From the uterine tube the ovum travels into the womb or uterus. This is a hollow bag made of muscle, with a thick, soft lining of blood vessels. If the ovum is fertilized, it can embed itself in the lining of the uterus and start to grow.

**4** If the egg is not fertilized, it passes through the vagina. This is a stretchy tube leading from the uterus to the outside of a woman's body.

## Sperm

Sperm are tiny tadpole-shaped cells, which are produced and stored inside a man's testicles (also called testes). They are made in great quantities, about 200 million or more maturing each day. The testicles hang outside a man's body in a loose pouch of skin called the scrotum. There is a tube down the middle of the penis which carries urine from the bladder out of the body. The testicles are connected to this by tubes called sperm ducts.

**Bladder**

**Sperm duct**

**Scrotum**

**Penis**

**Testicles (testes)**

## The journey of the sperm

1 When a man and a woman have sexual intercourse, a man's penis fits into a woman's vagina. At the climax of intercourse for the man (male orgasm), the sperm travel from their storage place in the testicles through the sperm ducts to the penis.

2 As the sperm travel through the ducts, fluids are added to them to produce a mixture called semen. During the orgasm the semen is squirted out (ejaculated) from the penis into the woman's vagina.

3 From the vagina the sperm swim up into the uterus and from there to the uterine tubes. One ejaculation contains about 300 million sperm, but only about 1,000 get as far as the tubes before they die.

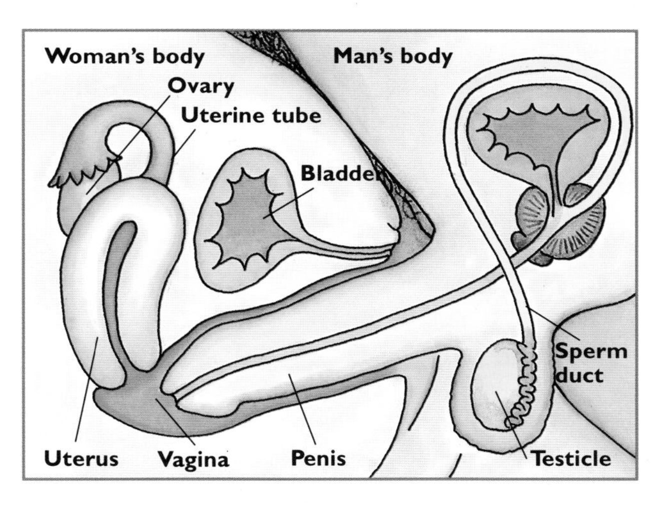


4 If the sperm meet an ovum in one of the uterine tubes, they all cluster around it and try to break through the outer layer that surrounds it. As soon as one sperm breaks through, it fuses with the ovum to form a new cell. The rest of the sperm cannot now enter the ovum and will die.

## The new cell starts growing

The new cell, formed when the ovum and sperm join together, divides to form two identical cells. These two divide to make four, the four divide to make eight, and so on, until a solid ball of cells is formed.

The ball of cells continues to travel down the uterine tube. When it reaches the uterus, it embeds itself in the lining. This is called implantation and usually happens seven to 10 days after fertilization. Once this has happened, the woman is pregnant.

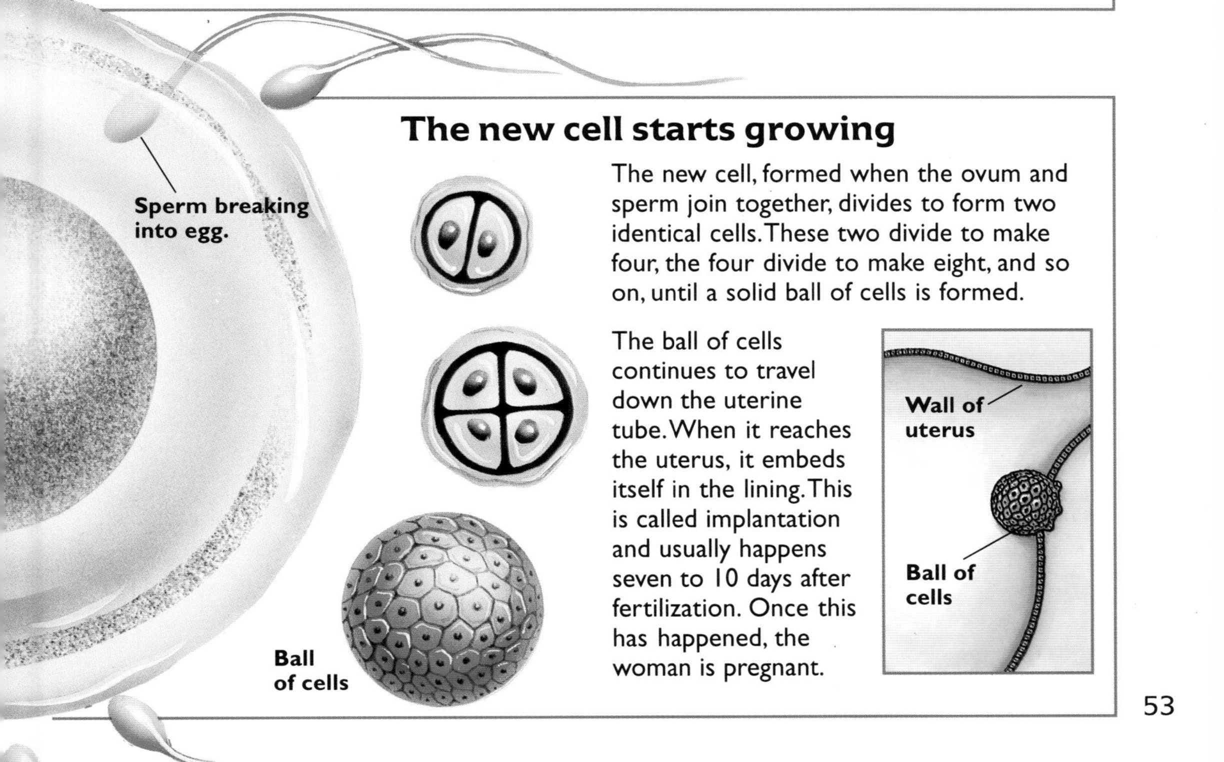

## When can a woman become pregnant?

For a woman to become pregnant, a live sperm must meet one of her egg cells while it is moving along one of her uterine tubes. She usually produces only one ripened egg cell each month. This is normally released about two weeks before the start of her period.* It takes a day for it to travel along the tube from her ovary to her uterus.

Sperm can survive inside a woman's uterus for about five days. There are therefore about six "fertile" days each month (five days before the egg is released and one after), when a woman may become pregnant if she has sexual intercourse without using any form of contraception (way of preventing pregnancy).

Avoiding sexual intercourse during the fertile days each month is not a reliable way to avoid getting pregnant. This is mainly because it is difficult to know exactly when ovulation is going to happen. Even women who have a regular, 28-day period cycle do not always ovulate at the expected time. It is possible for a baby to be conceived at any point during the period cycle.

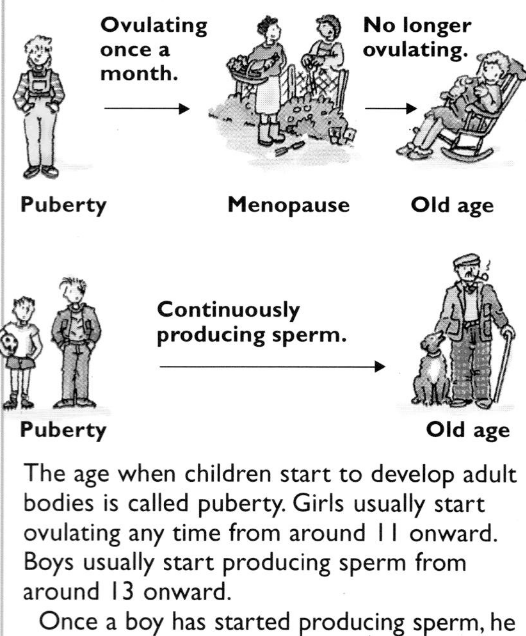


The age when children start to develop adult bodies is called puberty. Girls usually start ovulating any time from around 11 onward. Boys usually start producing sperm from around 13 onward.

Once a boy has started producing sperm, he goes on producing them continuously, not just once a month, throughout his life. Women usually stop ovulating at around 50. This time is known as the menopause or "change of life".

**An average period lasts four or five days.** (period: days 1–4, week 1)

**Sperm entering the uterus during this time will have a chance of fertilizing the egg. This is often called the "fertile time".** (week 2)

**Ovum released (ovulation).**

**Ovum travels down uterine tube.**

**When the ovum is released, the lining of the uterus thickens and softens, ready for the ovum to nestle in, if it is fertilized by a sperm.** (week 3)

**If the ovum is fertilized, about seven days later it implants itself in the lining of the uterus.**

**If the ovum is not fertilized, the lining of the uterus starts to disintegrate.** (week 4)

**If the ovum has implanted itself in the lining of the uterus, the woman is pregnant and does not have a period.**

**If the ovum has not been fertilized, two weeks after its release, the lining of the uterus, mixed with blood, passes out of the woman's body as a period.** (period; week 5)

| Day |
|---|
| 1 |
| 2 |
| 3 |
| 4 |
| 5 |
| 6 |
| 7 |
| 8 |
| 9 |
| 10 |
| 11 |
| 12 |
| 13 |
| 14 |
| 15 |
| 16 |
| 17 |
| 18 |
| 19 |
| 20 |
| 21 |
| 22 |
| 23 |
| 24 |
| 25 |
| 26 |
| 27 |
| 28 |
| 29 |
| 30 |
| 31 |
| 32 |
| 33 |
| 34 |



*To find out more about periods, see pages 20-23.

## First signs that a baby is developing

Once a fertilized egg has implanted itself in a woman's uterus, changes start to take place in her body, from which she can tell that she may be pregnant. These are some early signs:

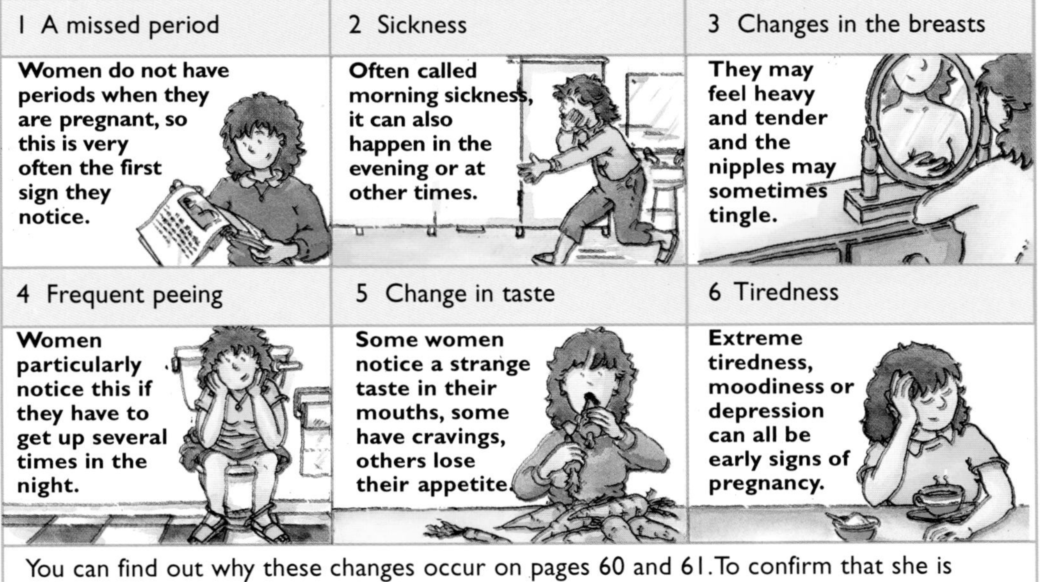


You can find out why these changes occur on pages 60 and 61. To confirm that she is pregnant, a woman needs to have a pregnancy test.

## Pregnancy tests

One of the main ways of confirming that a woman is pregnant is to test a sample of her urine with chemicals. The chemicals can detect certain substances which the body produces only in pregnancy.

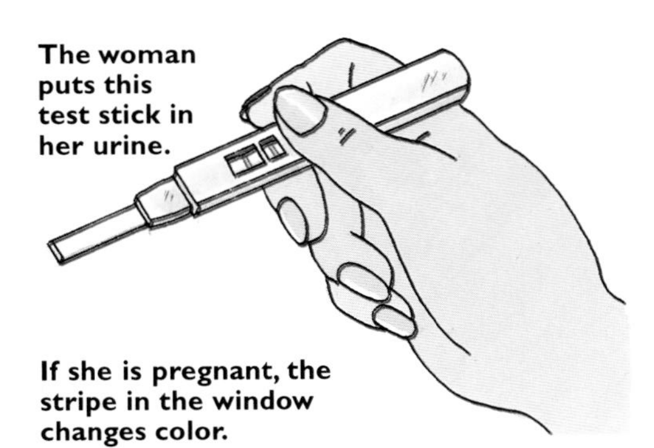


The woman can do the test herself with a kit from the pharmacy, or a doctor or birth control clinic can do it for her. Some tests work as early as the first day of a missed period, although a second test may be done later to make absolutely sure.

## Planning the pregnancy

A pregnant woman discusses with her doctor or midwife the type of care she will have during her pregnancy and where the baby will be born. A midwife is a specialist in pregnancy and birth.

## Phantom pregnancy

In some very rare cases, a woman can become absolutely convinced that she is pregnant even when she is not. She shows clear signs of pregnancy, including missed periods and putting on weight. This is known as a phantom pregnancy.

# How a baby grows inside its mother

A baby grows very rapidly inside its mother. In the first 10 weeks after its conception, it develops from a single cell into something that is recognizable as a human being. By the time it is ready to be born, it will have approximately 200 million cells. During the first 10 weeks, the developing baby is referred to as an embryo. After that it is called a fetus.

## When will the baby be born?

Most babies stay inside their mothers for about 38 weeks before they are born. But because the exact date when the egg and sperm met is not usually known, the pregnancy is dated from the first day of the mother's last period, which makes it 40 weeks (10 months) long. This is roughly equal to nine calendar months (January, February etc.,) plus one extra week. Doctors usually use a chart or disk to help them determine the "expected delivery date".

## The first three months

| 0 weeks | 1 week | 2 weeks | 3 weeks | 4 weeks | 5 weeks |
|---|---|---|---|---|---|
| First day of last period | | Egg is fertilized. | Egg implants in lining of uterus. | Missed period | Embryo just big enough to be visible. |

**6 weeks**

**7 weeks**

At eight weeks, the embryo has eyes but no eyelids. It starts making its first tiny movements but its mother cannot feel them yet.

By 12 weeks, the baby is easily recognizable as a human being, although its head is still very large in proportion to the rest of its body. Girls and boys start to look distinctly different from each other at about this stage.

**8 weeks**

**12 weeks**

At six weeks, the beginnings of a backbone and brain are forming. The heart starts to beat.

At seven weeks, four tiny swellings have developed. These are the beginnings of hands and feet.

# The baby's life support system

The human body needs food and oxygen in order to stay alive and grow. It also has to get rid of waste products. While a baby is inside its mother, it does not eat or breathe, but gets its food and oxygen from its mother's blood. Waste products are transferred from its blood to its mother's. This exchange of substances between the mother's blood and the baby's happens via a special organ called a placenta.

When the embryo first sticks to the lining of the uterus, it dissolves some of the cells beneath it, sinks inward and starts to feed off its mother's blood. It gradually grows a network of blood vessels. This mixes with a network of blood vessels grown by its mother. The two networks mixed together form the placenta. It is fully developed by the time the embryo is about 10 weeks old.

The baby is attached to the placenta by a cord leading out of its navel. This is called an umbilical cord. Blood, carrying food and oxygen, travels from the placenta through the cord to the baby's body. It travels around the baby's body and back to the placenta. On its way back it carries waste products from the baby's body. From the placenta they pass into the mother's blood.

The blood vessels of the mother and baby do not actually join each other but have a thin layer of cells separating them. This acts as a barrier and helps to prevent some, but not all, harmful substances getting through to the baby.

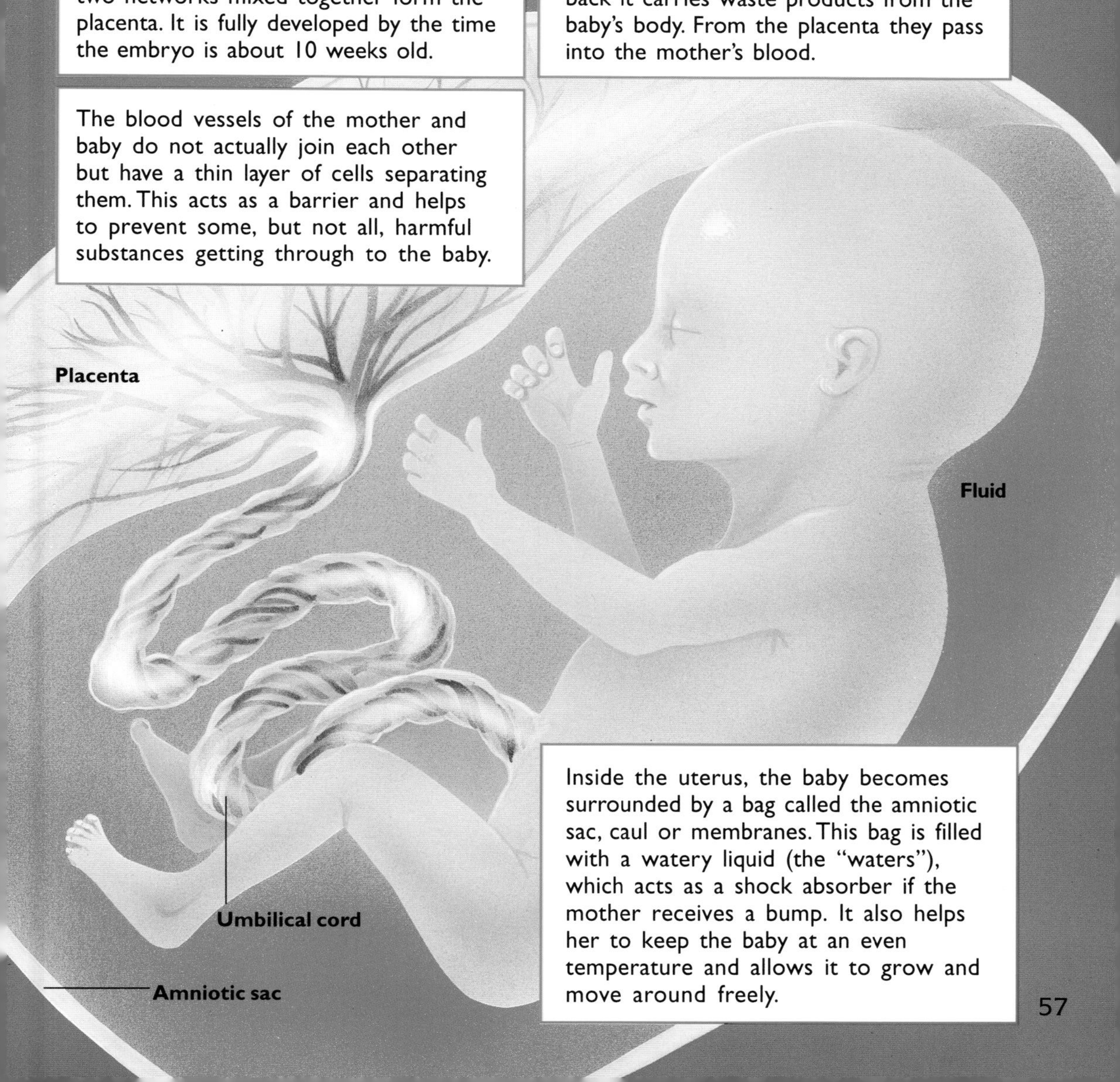

Inside the uterus, the baby becomes surrounded by a bag called the amniotic sac, caul or membranes. This bag is filled with a watery liquid (the "waters"), which acts as a shock absorber if the mother receives a bump. It also helps her to keep the baby at an even temperature and allows it to grow and move around freely.

## 16 weeks (4 months)*

The uterus is now entirely filled by the baby, placenta and waters, and gradually stretches from now on as the baby continues to grow. The baby begins to swallow and to pass urine. It has finger and toenails. At this stage its skin is bright red and transparent.

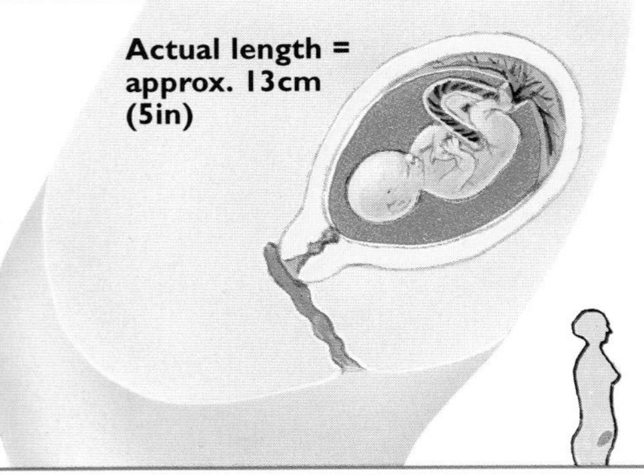


The mother's bulge is just beginning to show and her clothes are getting tight. Any sickness she was feeling earlier has usually gone by this time.

## 20 weeks (5 months)

The baby's hair is starting to appear and it now has eyebrows and eyelashes. Its eyes are still tightly closed and the whole surface of its body is covered with a fine, downy hair called lanugo. Its skin is now less transparent but very wrinkled.

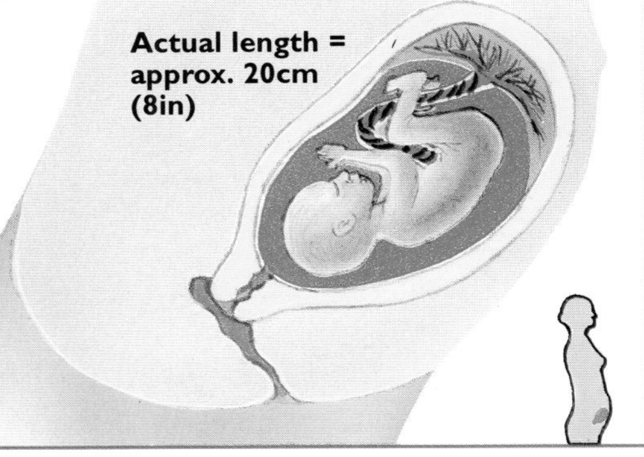


Sometime between about 18 and 22 weeks, the mother usually begins to feel her baby moving when it wiggles around and exercises its arms and legs.

## 24 weeks (6 months)

The baby now has distinct periods of sleep and wakefulness. It can probably hear voices, music and other sounds from outside its mother, above the noise of her heartbeat and blood circulating. If the baby were born now, it would have a chance of surviving, provided it received expert care in a special premature baby unit.

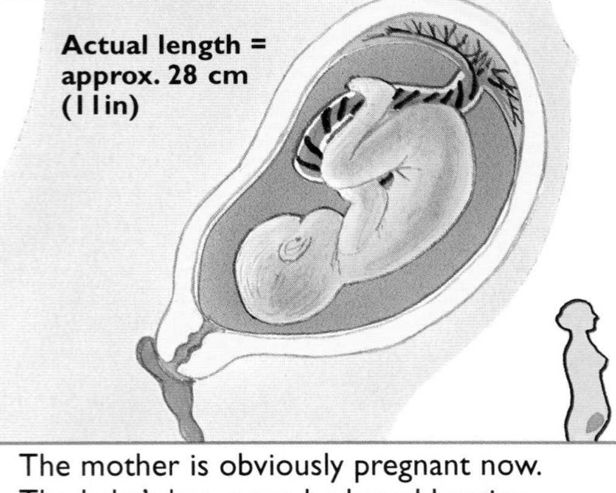


The mother is obviously pregnant now. The baby's heart can be heard beating through a special listening device called a fetal stethoscope.

## 28 weeks (7 months)

If the baby were born at this stage, it would have a good chance of surviving, but it would have to be put in an incubator because its lungs are still not well enough developed for it to breathe on its own. The baby is now covered with a thick, white grease called vernix, which helps to prevent its skin from becoming waterlogged.

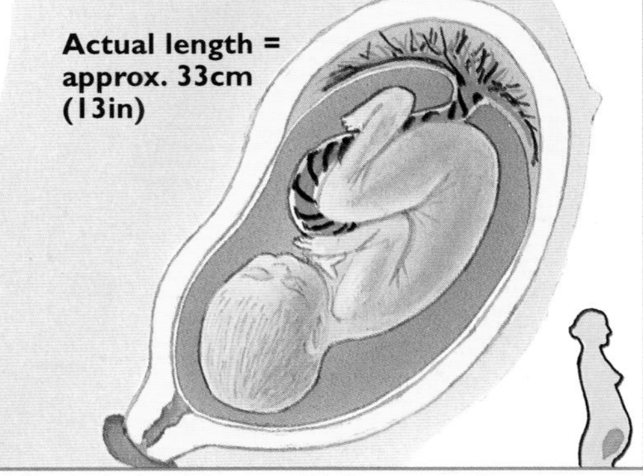


The baby's kicks are fairly strong by now and can be felt by putting a hand on the mother's tummy. Sometimes she can feel her baby having hiccups.



*Dated from the first day of the mother's last period.*

## 32 weeks (8 months)

The baby starts to put on some fat and become less wrinkled. Its lungs are starting to mature and get ready to take their first breath. It may begin to try sucking - some babies suck their thumbs before they are born.

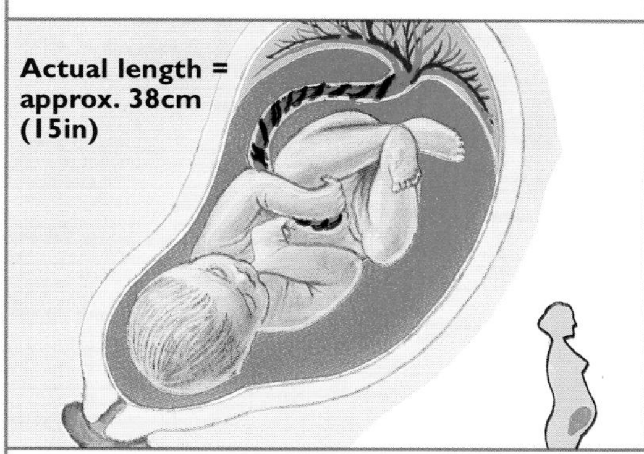


The mother may lean back noticeably by now to counteract the baby's weight and she may walk with her legs slightly apart to help her balance.

## 36 weeks (9 months)

By now the baby has usually taken up its final position in the uterus - usually head down. From now on, it has no room to somersault around because it fills the uterus, which cannot expand any more. It continues to get fatter.

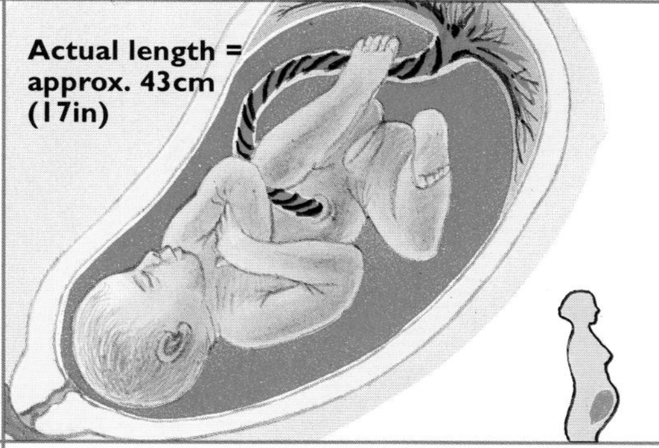


You may be able to see the mother's tummy moving when the baby moves its limbs. Often you can guess whether the bump is a hand or a foot.

## 40 weeks (10 months)

Some time from 36 weeks onward, the baby's head drops down into its mother's pelvis, or "engages", ready for the birth.

**Actual length = approx. 50cm (20in)**

**Pelvis**

When the baby's head engages, the mother may be able to breathe more easily, as her lungs have been getting squashed and this allows them a little more room.

The time when the baby is fully ready to be born is referred to as "full term" or "term". 40 weeks is only an average length of pregnancy and it is perfectly normal for a baby to arrive any time between the 38th and 42nd week.

By this time the lanugo has usually disappeared, except perhaps from the shoulders, but the baby's body may still be covered with vernix.

# Changes in the mother's body

When a woman is pregnant, her body undergoes a whole range of changes, adapting itself to the needs of the growing baby and preparing itself for the birth. These changes are triggered by special chemicals called hormones, which travel around her body in her blood.

The main hormones of pregnancy are progesterone and estrogen. These are present in all women's bodies, but in pregnancy they are produced in much greater quantities than usual. They are normally produced by the ovaries, but after the first three months of pregnancy the placenta takes over this job.

## The uterus

One of the most obvious changes during pregnancy is that the mother's uterus gets much bigger to make room for the growing baby inside it. The uterus is made of a type of muscle called smooth muscle. The hormone, progesterone, has the effect of relaxing smooth muscle and making it more stretchy so that it can expand more easily. Here you can see the size of the uterus at different stages of pregnancy.

## The breasts

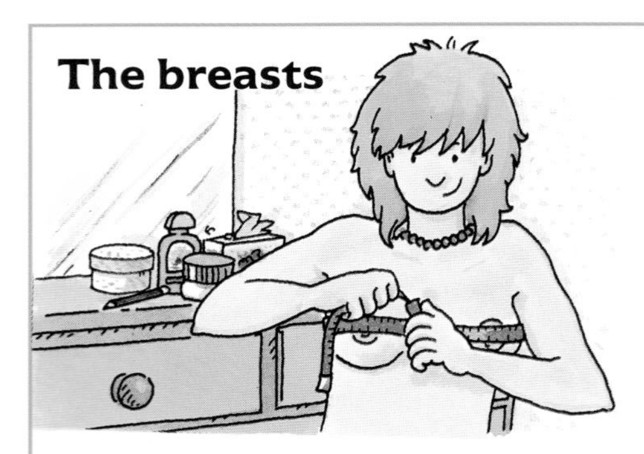

The hormones of pregnancy start preparing the breasts to produce milk and they increase considerably in size. They start making a substance called colostrum but do not produce any milk until about two or three days after the baby is born (see pages 82-83).

## The pelvis

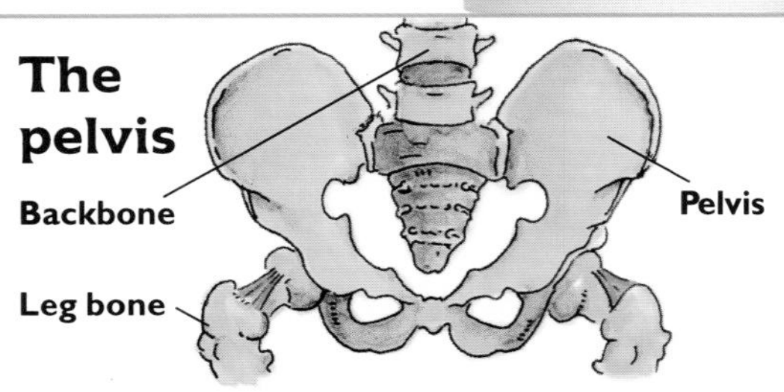


The pelvis is the circle of bone which connects the leg bones to the bottom of the spine. It is actually made of three bones joined together by tough fibers called ligaments. When a baby is born, it has to pass through the bottom of this circle. During pregnancy, progesterone makes the ligaments softer and more stretchy, so that the pelvis can expand and let the baby through more easily.

## Some inconvenient side effects

Many women feel perfectly fit and healthy throughout pregnancy, but most experience at least one or two of the complaints listed here. They are mainly caused by the increase in the amount of hormones circulating in the woman's body and the increased size of the uterus, which puts pressure on other organs and extra weight at the front of the body.

Backache
Bad balance
Breathlessness
Clumsiness

**At 36 weeks - it reaches up as far as the breast bone (where the ribs join together at the front of the chest).**

**At 22 weeks - it reaches about the size of a football.**

**At 12 weeks - about the size of a grapefruit.**

**Before pregnancy - about the size of a small pear.**

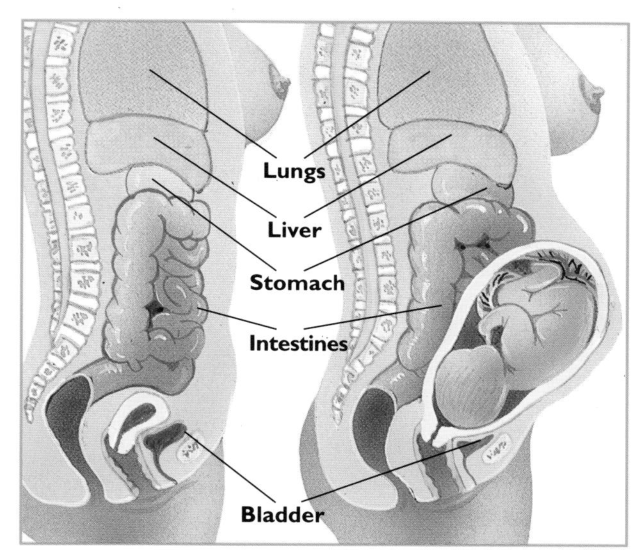


These two pictures show how the growth of the baby and the uterus squashes all the other things that normally fill the space inside the body.

## The skin

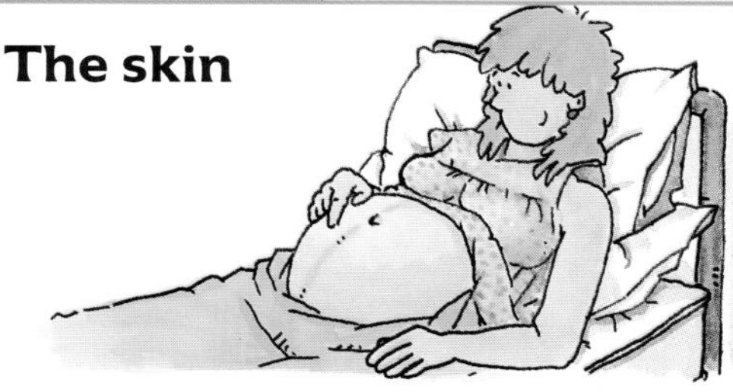

Pregnant women sometimes feel noticeably warmer than usual, due to the increase in the amount of blood passing through the blood vessels in their skin. Most pregnant women also find that their moles and freckles, and the area around their nipples, become darker brown, and a dark line, the "linea nigra", appears down the middle of their abdomen.* Occasionally, dark patches also appear on the face.

## The blood

**Liver** **Lungs**

**Intestines** **Kidneys** **Baby**

During pregnancy, the amount of blood in the mother's body can increase by as much as half, and her heart has to beat harder to pump the extra blood around her body. The extra blood helps to supply the needs of the baby and the mother's other organs, which all have to work harder than usual.

Constipation
Cramps
Emotional changes ("highs", "lows" or rapid mood changes)
Faintness
Forgetfulness
Frequent urination
Headaches
Heartburn (burning sensation in chest)
Itchy skin
Sleeplessness
Stretch marks (pink or blue lines on skin)
Swollen ankles, feet and hands
Varicose (swollen) veins in legs
Vivid dreams
Vomiting



*The abdomen is the part of the body between the chest and the top of the legs.*

# Making sure the mother and baby are healthy

Pregnancy is a natural process of the body. Many women feel perfectly fit and healthy throughout and can continue doing almost all the things they usually do. However, their bodies are under a lot of extra strain and it is important that they take good care of themselves. The health of a mother and her baby are very closely linked during pregnancy.

## Everyday activities

As the mother's body gets larger and the weight of the baby increases, there is a danger that the muscles in her abdomen may get overstretched. If they do, they cannot do their job properly and this may lead to backache. The loosening of the joints in the mother's body, brought about by hormones, also increases the likelihood of back problems. Whether sitting, standing, walking or lifting things, she should keep her back as straight as possible. She needs to be especially careful when doing any of the activities shown on the right.

**Lifting and carrying heavy weights: might cause back strain.**

**Leaning forward: might cause back strain.**

**Standing still for a long time: bad for blood circulation.**

**Balancing: balance not good, might fall.**

## Exercise, rest and relaxation

It is sensible for pregnant women to keep up any exercise they are used to. Special exercises to strengthen muscles and prepare the body to give birth can be helpful, as can exercises which help the body to relax. A tense body cannot rest properly and during pregnancy it is important to get plenty of rest.

## Going to classes

Classes offer people a chance to meet others in the same situation, discuss feelings, exchange information and learn about pregnancy, birth and becoming parents. They can also try out relaxation techniques and positions to help the mother during pregnancy and while giving birth.

## Putting on weight

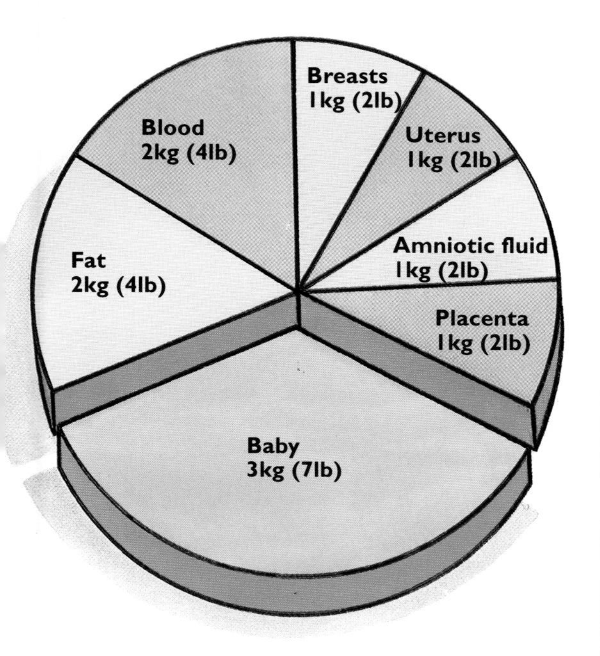


Most women gain between 9kg (approx. 20lbs) and 13kg (approx. 28lbs) while they are pregnant. The extra weight gain is made up roughly as shown in the chart above. As you can see, only a fairly small proportion of the extra weight is fat.

## Eating well

While a woman is pregnant, it is even more important than usual that she eats a healthy diet consisting of a wide variety of good, fresh food. The food she eats supplies her baby's needs as well as her own and the baby will take what it needs, even if this does not leave enough to keep the mother healthy. She will probably want to eat a little more than usual but may find that she can only eat small amounts at a time, especially toward the end of pregnancy, because her stomach is squashed into a smaller space.

## Things that can hurt an unborn baby

Just as food and oxygen can pass through the placenta to the unborn baby, so can other things which the mother takes into her body. Some of these can damage the baby, especially during the first three months of its existence, when its body is developing very rapidly. At this stage the parents often do not yet know that the baby is there. This is one reason why it is important for parents to plan pregnancies.

Many medicines and other drugs can pass through the placenta and some can be harmful. A pregnant woman should check with her doctor or midwife before she takes any medicines, even those she can buy without a prescription.

Babies of mothers who smoke tend to be underweight and have feeding problems, and are more at risk of catching certain infections when they are first born. There is also evidence to suggest that babies of fathers who smoke are more likely to experience these problems.

Alcohol crosses the placenta and should be avoided altogether in pregnancy or taken only in small amounts.

A few infectious diseases can damage a baby if its mother has them early in pregnancy. The most common one is German measles (rubella) which can affect a baby's heart, sight or hearing. Many girls and women are now immunized against rubella, but this must not be done during or immediately before a pregnancy.

# Medical checkups

Pregnant women need to have regular checkups to make sure that the baby is growing and developing normally, and to check that the mother is not developing any problems that might seriously affect her or the baby. The checkups may take place at a hospital, health clinic, doctor's office, or midwife's clinic. They are called antenatal ("before birth") checkups. Doctors specializing in pregnancy are called obstetricians. A midwife is a specialist in pregnancy but is not a doctor.

**1**

On her first visit to the doctor, a blood sample is taken and tested to check general health and detect any problems that might affect the baby. More blood tests are taken later in pregnancy.

**2**

A sample of the mother's urine is tested with chemicals at every visit. The presence of certain substances, such as sugar or protein, can give warning that problems are developing in her body.

**3**

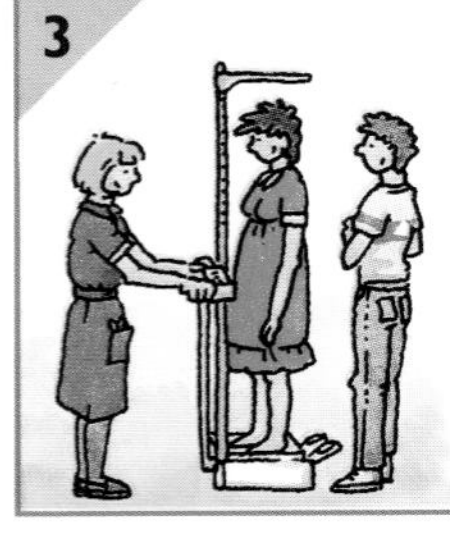

The mother's weight is checked regularly. After the first three months she should gain weight slowly but steadily. This is good for the growing baby and for breastfeeding.

**4**

At every visit her blood pressure (the force with which the heart pumps blood around the body) is measured. High blood pressure can affect the baby's growth and cause problems for the mother.

**5**

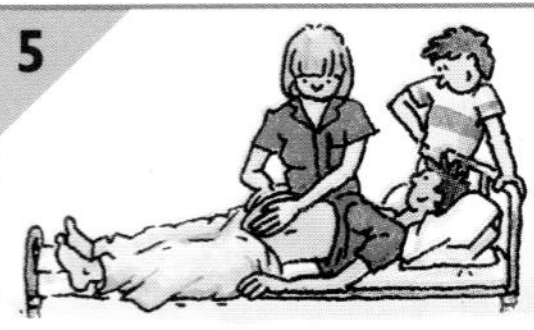

The doctor examines the mother's uterus by feeling it through her abdomen. Its size gives a good indication of how the baby is growing. Later in pregnancy, the doctor can feel the baby's position.

**6**

The baby's heartbeat is checked through a listening device called a fetal stethoscope. A special machine may be used which electronically amplifies the sound of the baby's heart.

# Ultrasound examination

This is a method of examining an unborn baby by sending sound waves, far above the range of human hearing, into the mother's body. The waves bounce back off the surfaces they meet inside the body and these echoes are measured and translated into dots of light. The dots are used to build up a picture of the baby on a screen similar to a TV screen.

This method can be used to assess the age, size and growth rate of a baby. It will also show whether the mother is going to have twins, long before she or her doctor would normally suspect they are there.

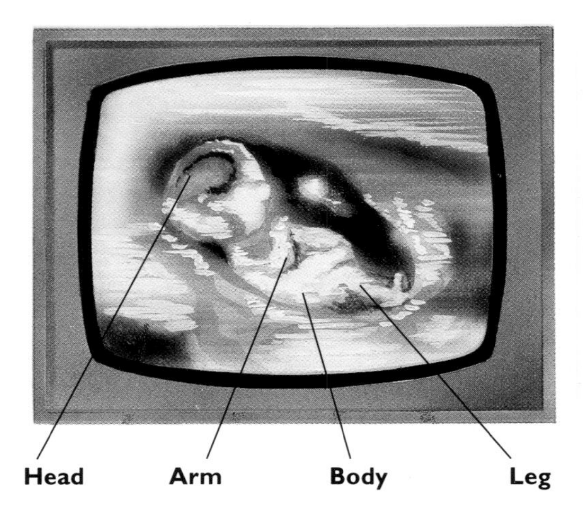

## Testing for abnormalities

Most babies are born perfectly healthy, but a small percentage have a physical or mental disability. There are a number of tests that can be done during pregnancy to see whether a baby has any problems. Blood tests and ultrasound examinations may indicate certain abnormalities. If they do, or there is a possibility that the baby may have inherited some abnormality, doctors may suggest doing one of the tests shown below. These tests are done with great care not to damage the baby.

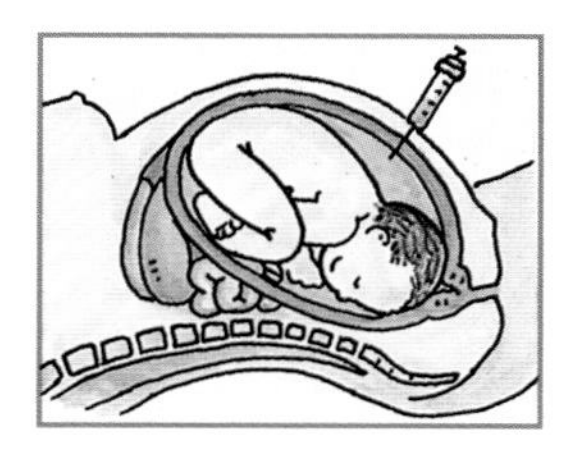

**1** The fluid in the amniotic sac surrounding the baby contains some of the baby's cells. Some of this fluid can be obtained by a method called amniocentesis. First the mother has an injection of local anesthetic to numb a small patch of skin on her abdomen. Then a hollow needle is passed through her skin into her uterus. A small sample of fluid is sucked out into a syringe attached to the end of the needle and sent to a laboratory for tests.

**2** One instrument designed to check the health of an unborn baby is called a fetoscope. It is a very small telescope mounted on the end of a hollow needle. When the needle is passed through the mother's abdomen and into her uterus, the doctor can look through it and see the baby. It is even possible to take photographs through a fetoscope.

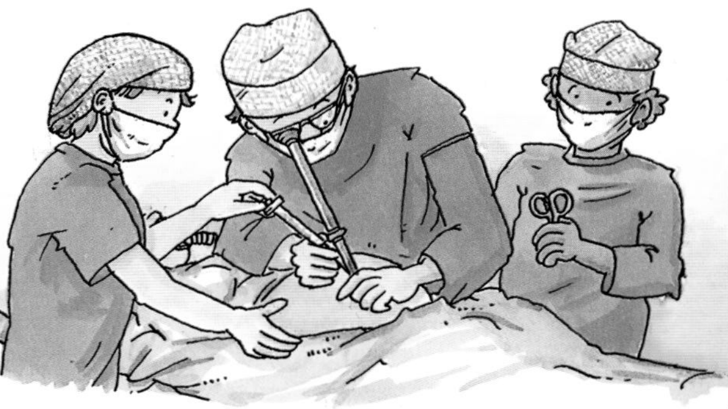

## Finding out what sex the baby will be

There are many myths about how to tell what sex a baby will be, but at present the only reliable method of prediction involves examining one of the baby's cells. If, for particular medical reasons, the mother has an amniocentesis, the doctors can tell whether she will have a boy or a girl. However, in many cases the parents ask not to be told.

### What is a miscarriage?

A baby born at the 24th week of pregnancy stands a chance of surviving. A baby born earlier than this usually dies. This is known as a miscarriage. There are many reasons why miscarriages may happen and often the cause is not known. They are unfortunately very common, especially in the early stages of pregnancy. It is thought that many early miscarriages happen because the baby is not developing normally. A miscarriage is sometimes referred to as a "spontaneous abortion".

### What is an abortion?

If the doctors have reason to believe that a baby is likely to be seriously mentally or physically disabled, or that the mother could be badly damaged physically or mentally by continuing with a pregnancy, the parents sometimes decide that it would be better if the baby did not survive. If they do, the mother goes into a hospital or clinic and the baby is removed from her uterus. This is called an abortion or "termination of pregnancy".

# How a baby is born

The process by which a baby leaves its mother's uterus and emerges into the world is called labor or childbirth. It happens in three stages. Nobody knows exactly what causes labor to start. Most evidence suggests that when a baby has reached the point where it is ready to be born, it produces hormones which reach its mother's body through the placenta and trigger it into labor.

The length of time that labor lasts varies immensely. The average time for a first baby is about 12-15 hours, but it can be much longer or much shorter than this. The time tends to get shorter with each baby a woman has.

## First stage

During the first stage of labor, the bottom part of the uterus opens up enough to give the baby room to get out. This part of the uterus, which separates it from the vagina, is called the cervix. In the middle of the cervix there is a tiny opening or passage, which is normally only about 2mm wide.

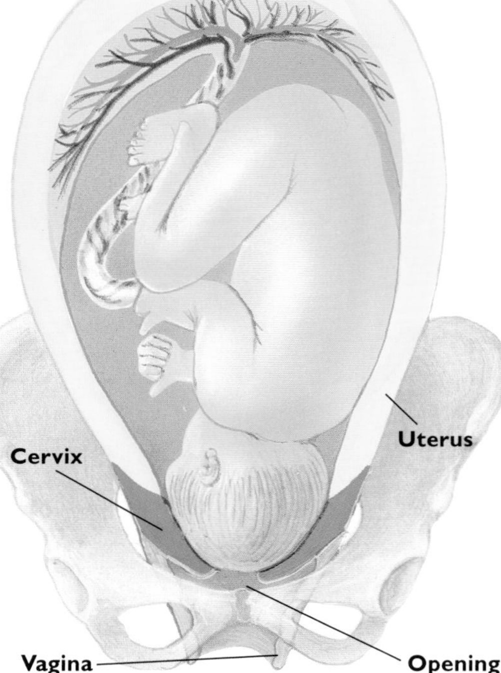


At the end of pregnancy, the uterus is the largest and one of the most powerful muscles in the body. During labor the muscle in the upper part of the uterus keeps contracting (becoming smaller) and then relaxing again. The contractions gradually pull the cervix open. After each contraction the uterus remains slightly smaller than it was before, so the baby's head becomes firmly pressed against the cervix, helping it to open up.

The average diameter of a newborn baby's head is 9.5cm (approx. 4in), so the opening in the cervix has to reach about 10cm to allow it to go through. At some point the pressure on the bag of waters surrounding the baby becomes so great that the bag breaks. The fluid runs out through the cervix and vagina.

## Contractions

The first stage is the longest part of labor. The average length for a first baby is about 10 hours. In early labor the contractions may be 20 or 30 minutes apart, but as the labor progresses they gradually get more frequent and stronger. By the time the cervix is fully opened, the uterus will be contracting about every two minutes and the contractions lasting about one and a half minutes.

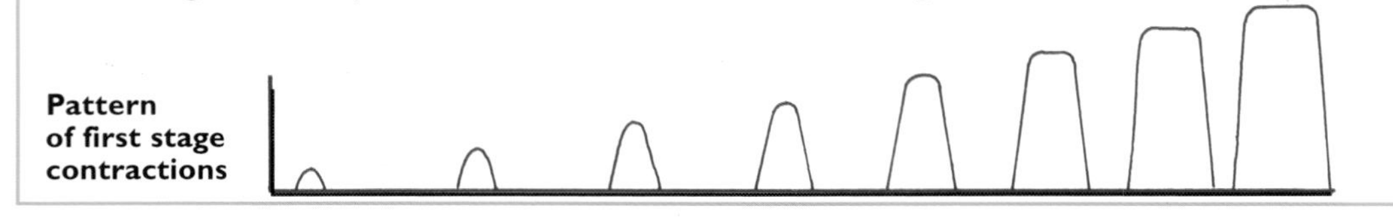

## Second stage

The second stage of labor starts when the cervix is fully open and ends with the baby actually being born or "delivered". This stage may take anything from a few minutes to about two hours.

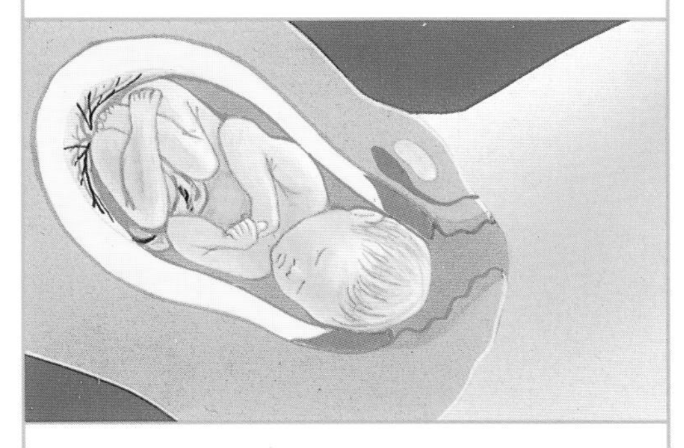

Between leaving the uterus and emerging from its mother's body, the baby travels through the vagina or "birth canal". The walls of the vagina have folds or pleats in them, so when the baby passes through they can expand to make room.

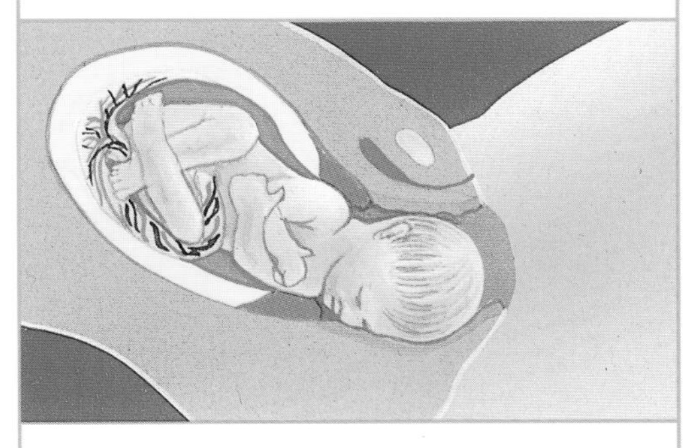

The uterus continues to contract at regular intervals and during the contractions the mother feels an urge to use her muscles to push the baby out. Once the baby's head has passed out of the vagina, the rest of its body usually slips out fairly easily.

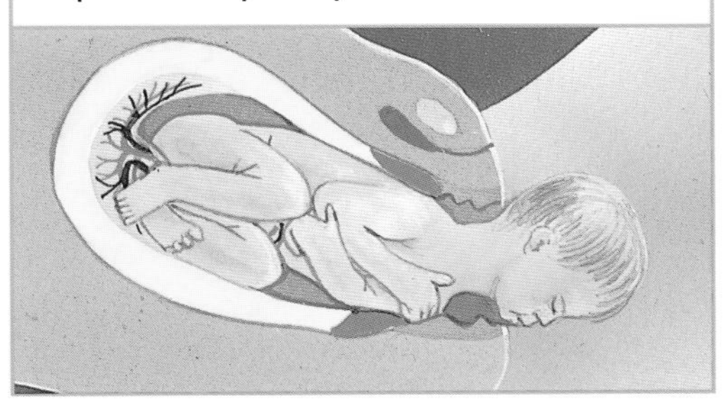

## Third stage

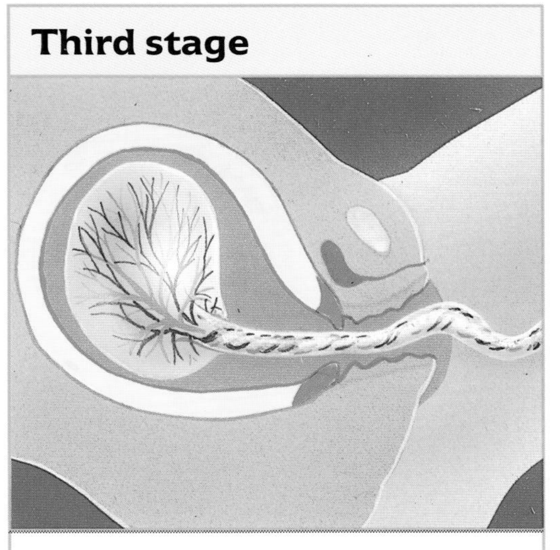

When the baby is born, it is still attached to the placenta by its umbilical cord, and the placenta is still attached to the wall of the uterus. Shortly after the birth, the placenta detaches itself from the uterus and passes through the vagina and out of the mother's body. The empty amniotic sac, which is still attached to the placenta, comes with it. The placenta, the sac and the cord are sometimes called the "afterbirth".

## How does the mother know labor is starting?

For the mother, the first sign that labor is starting may be when she becomes aware of cramp-like pains coming at regular intervals, perhaps 20 or 30 minutes apart. They are caused by the contractions of her uterus and are usually felt low down in the abdomen or at the bottom of the back. She may also notice the whole of her abdomen tightening during the contractions.

Sometimes the bag of waters bursts before she notices any contractions, and she feels fluid running out of her vagina.

When she goes to the toilet, she may notice that a small lump of mucus has passed out of her body. (This is known as a "show".) It has acted as a plug in the middle of her cervix throughout pregnancy, but when the cervix starts to open, it drops out.

## Checking the progress of labor

Even though a mother is under the care of a doctor, she is usually looked after by a nurse during labor. The nurse helps and encourages her and does regular checks to make sure everything is going well.

The nurse can check how the labor is progressing by feeling with her fingers inside the vagina how far the cervix has opened. When it reaches nearly 10cm (4in), she knows that the first stage is coming to an end. She may also want to check the mother's pulse, temperature and blood pressure from time to time.

By feeling the mother's abdomen, the nurse can check the timing and strength of the contractions and by listening to the baby's heartbeat, she can tell how the baby is. Occasionally the baby can get short of oxygen, which could be dangerous.

Hospitals have machines called monitors, which can be used to record the baby's heartbeat. The monitor shown in this picture is a portable one. When the transducer is held on the mother's abdomen, the baby's heartbeat is heard through the loudspeaker of the audio unit. Some larger, non-portable monitors record the contractions as well as the heartbeat.

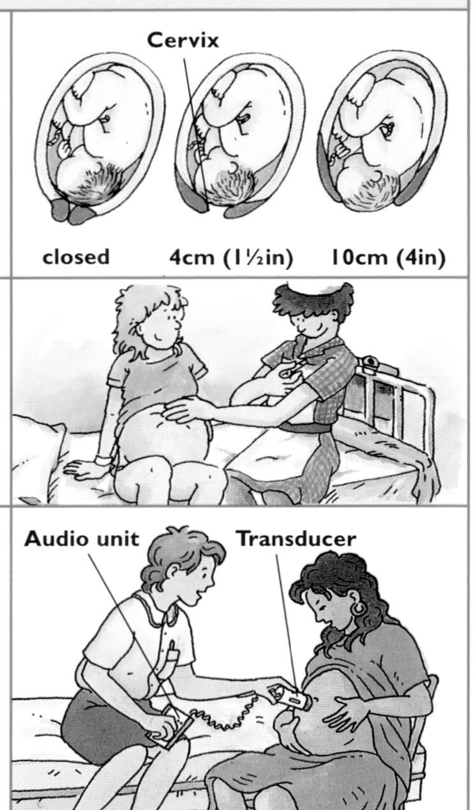


## What happens when the baby is born?

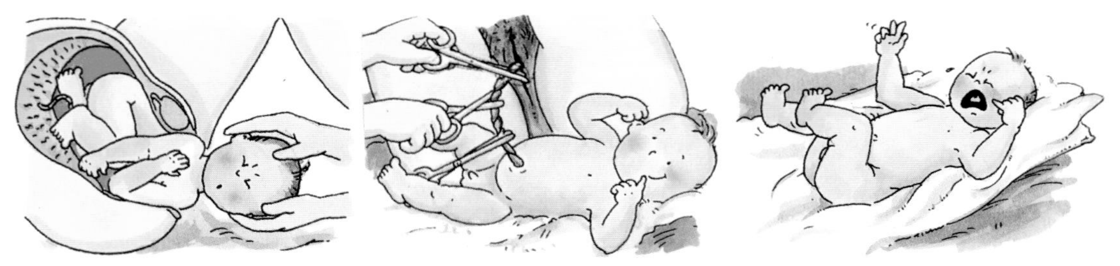

Most babies are born head first. When the chest is born, the baby can expand its lungs and start to breathe. Once the rest of the body has emerged, the doctor checks that its mouth and nose are clear of liquid.

At this stage, the baby is still attached to the placenta by its umbilical cord and the placenta is still inside the mother. After a few minutes, the cord is clamped in two places and then cut between the clamps.

The mother and father can then hold and cuddle their baby and take a good look at it. Some babies cry a lot soon after they are born, some very little or not at all. Crying can help them to fill their lungs with air and clear them of fluid.

## Helping the mother

Having a baby is a very exciting experience but it can also be painful and exhausting. Contractions are also known as "labor pains". Although they usually start as a fairly mild aching sensation, they become more painful as they get more frequent and stronger throughout the first stage. The end of the first stage is generally the most painful time of the whole labor. The second stage is very hard work for the mother and by the time the baby is born, she is often quite exhausted. Many fathers now share the experience with the mother and see their babies born. They can give a great deal of help and encouragement. There are several things that can be done to make the experience less painful.

**1** Pain feels much worse when you are tense. If the mother can breathe steadily and evenly during contractions and relax her body between them, it helps to reduce her tension and pain. Massage may help her to relax.

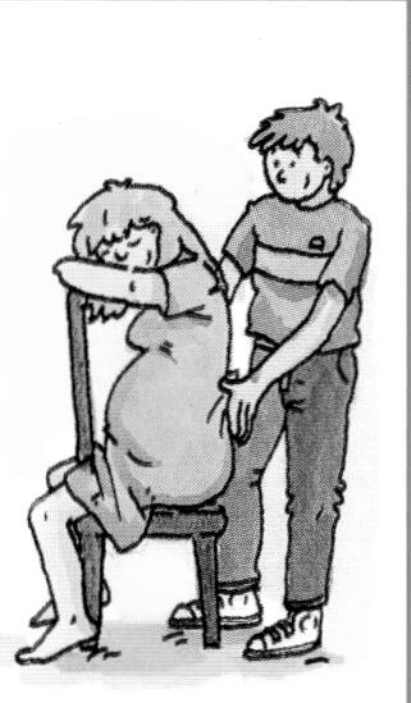

**2** If she wants, she can have an injection of a pain-relieving drug. As well as relieving her pain, the drug may make her drowsy. It can also cross the placenta and may make the baby a little drowsy when it is born.

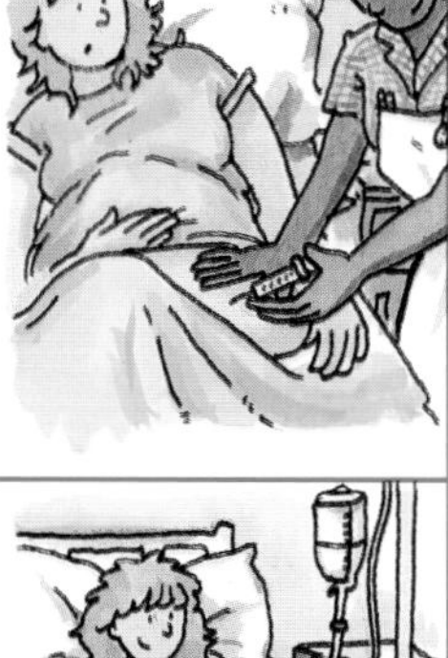

**3** She can choose to have some "gas and air". This is a mixture of nitrous oxide (laughing gas) and oxygen, which she breathes in through a mask every time she gets a contraction.

**4** She can have an "epidural block". This is an injection of local anesthetic into her back, which numbs the nerves around her spine and takes away all feeling from the lower half of her body.

After being checked to see that everything is normal, the baby is weighed and its length and head size are measured. It is important to know its birth weight as, from now on, regular weight checks are the best way of telling that it is growing well.

It is very important to keep the baby warm. Babies can lose heat rapidly, especially from their wet heads. After being cuddled by their parents, weighed and perhaps given a bath, they must be wrapped up warm.

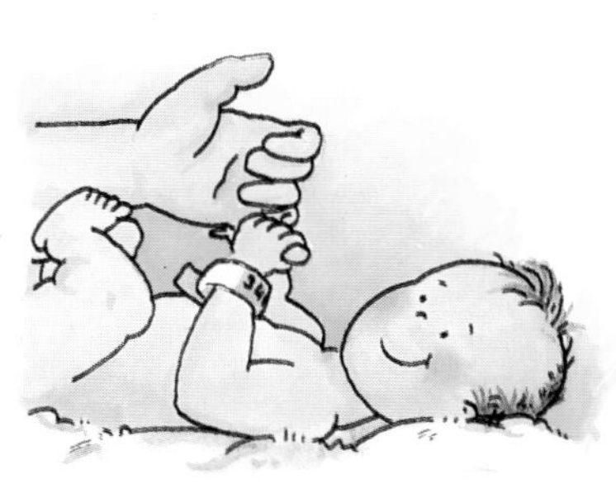

If a baby is born in the hospital, it has a label attached to its wrist, giving its name and the date and time it was born. The mother may have a matching label attached to her wrist. This avoids any confusion about who the baby belongs to.

## Helping to start labor

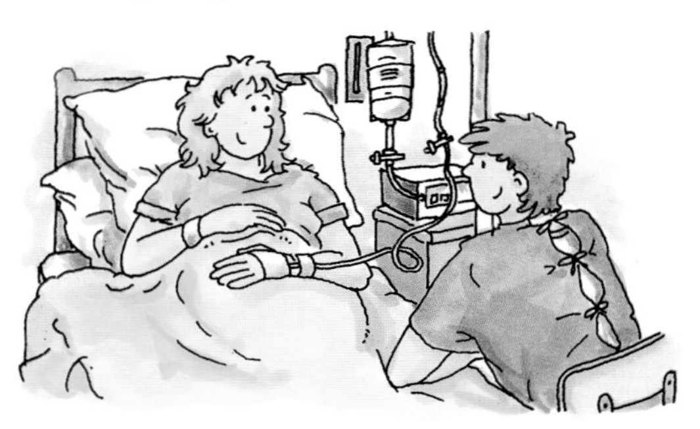

Sometimes the medical staff looking after a pregnant woman may think it advisable to start her labor off artificially rather than waiting for it to happen naturally. This is called "inducing" labor. They usually do this by giving her hormones, either in a special tablet (suppository) which dissolves when placed in her vagina, or in a fluid dripped into a vein in her arm via a needle (this method is usually referred to as "a drip").

## Using forceps to help with the birth

Sometimes the doctor needs to use forceps to speed up the second stage of labor. If this stage goes on too long, the baby may get short of oxygen. The ends of the forceps fit closely around the baby's head and the doctor gently pulls the baby out. Instead of using forceps, a doctor may use a suction device called a vacuum extractor or Ventouse.*

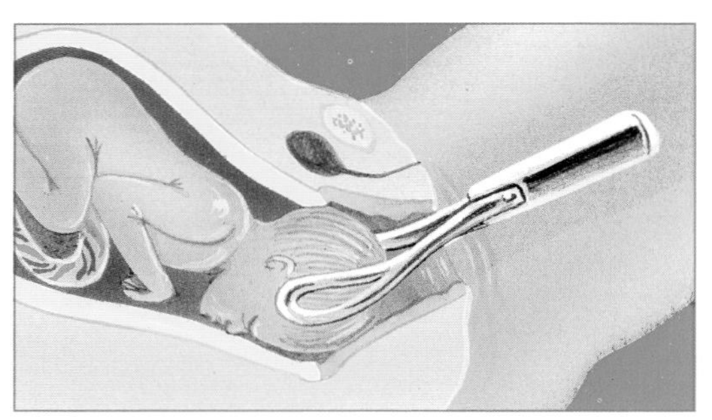

## Cutting and stitching

Sometimes the skin and muscle around the entrance to the vagina tears, when it stretches to let the baby's head through. A cut may be made to prevent this from happening. If forceps are used or the baby is in the breech position (see next page), a cut is nearly always made. After the birth, tears and cuts are repaired with stitches. They can be fairly sore for several days after the birth.

## Babies who need special care

Some babies are born needing special care. There are a number of reasons why this may be necessary. The baby may be premature (born more than three weeks before the expected date), or particularly small and light, or it may have some infection or defect. A baby like this is usually put in an incubator (an enclosed, transparent crib) and given special attention by doctors and nurses. Most babies who need special medical care during the first few days or weeks of their lives, grow into normal, healthy babies.

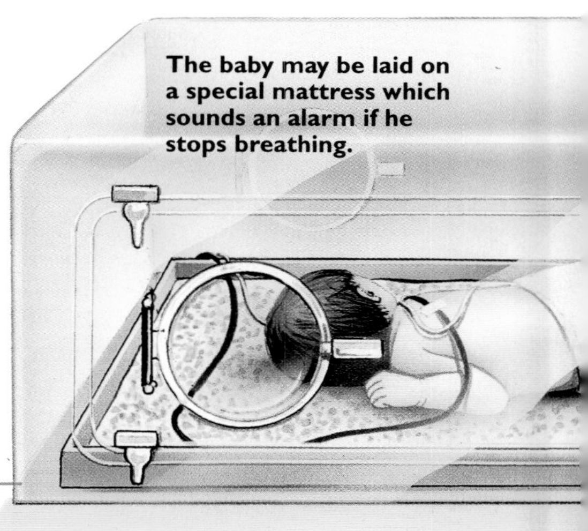

**The baby may be laid on a special mattress which sounds an alarm if he stops breathing.**



*Suction is applied via a metal cup placed on the baby's head.*

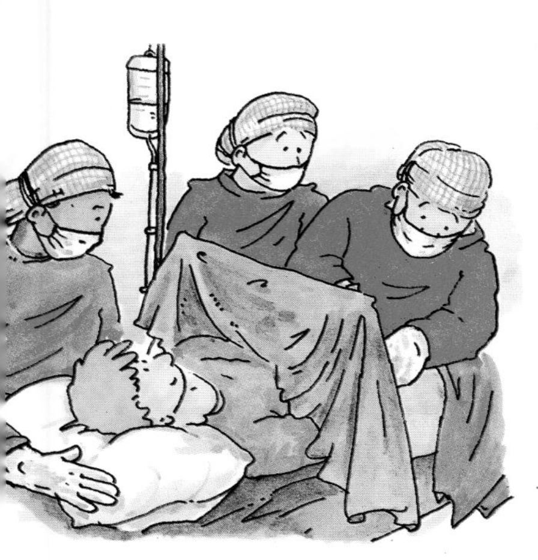

## What is a Caesarian birth?

A Caesarian is a method of delivering a baby by cutting through the mother's abdomen and uterus and lifting the baby and placenta out. The complete operation takes about 40 minutes. The mother may have a general anesthetic so that she is asleep during it, but it is fairly common to have an epidural block (see page 69) instead. This numbs the lower half of the mother's body so she can stay awake to see her baby born without feeling any pain.

A Caesarian is necessary if the baby cannot get out of the uterus because its mother's pelvis is too small or the placenta is blocking its path. It is also needed if the health of the mother or baby is at risk unless the baby is born quickly.

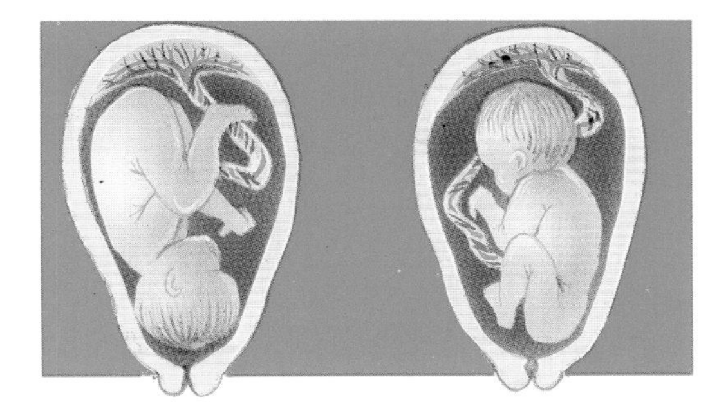

## What is a breech birth?

Most babies are born head first but a few do not turn into this position before labor starts and are born bottom or "breech" first. The birth is a little more difficult if the baby is in this position.

## Natural childbirth

Giving birth is a natural process for a woman's body but it does carry some risks for both mothers and babies. In an attempt to make childbirth safer there has been a move toward delivering most babies in a hospital. Over the last 30 years, there have also been developments in technology, so that labor can now be artificially started, speeded up, made less painful and more easily monitored.

There are disadvantages to the use of too much technology, however, and many people, including doctors and midwives, feel that it is better only to intervene in the natural course of events in labor for very specific medical reasons. They feel that the more a woman and her partner know about what happens in labor, how to help its progress and what medical help is available, the more satisfying and rewarding the experience will be. This attitude toward labor is sometimes referred to as the "natural childbirth movement".

**The temperature inside the incubator is carefully controlled. The baby does not need to wear anything except a diaper and can be observed more easily without clothes.**

**He may be fed by passing a tube through his nose and down into his stomach, or through an IV into a vein.**

**He can quickly be given extra oxygen if necessary.**

## What is a stillbirth?

A stillbirth is the birth of a dead baby after more than 24 weeks of pregnancy.* This is always a very sad event for the baby's parents and family but, in Western countries, it is now much less common than it used to be. This is due to improvements in the medical care of pregnant women and the early detection of possible problems affecting either the baby or the mother.

**Before this, it is a miscarriage or abortion (see page 65).*

# What makes a baby like it is?

From the instant of conception, when an ovum and a sperm join together inside the mother's body to form one new cell, that cell already contains all the information needed to construct a new and unique human being. The instructions inside each cell that tell the body how to develop are called genes. The way a person develops does not depend on genes alone. The people and things that surround them, their food and climate all influence their development as well.

**Nucleus**

**Cell**

**Chromosome (contains thousands of genes)**

**Cytoplasm**

**1** The human body starts as just one cell which, by dividing again and again, very quickly develops into billions of cells. Most of the cells in the body are so tiny that they can only be seen through a microscope. Each cell consists of a jelly-like substance called cytoplasm, with a nucleus in the middle. The nucleus contains thread-like structures called chromosomes. Each chromosome is made up of thousands of genes.

**2** Genes are like an incredibly complicated computer, which can store and classify very detailed information. Each gene is made up of chemicals joined together to look similar to a twisted ladder. The order of the chemicals in the rungs of the ladder varies and forms a code. A sequence of about 250 rungs gives the instructions for one particular characteristic such as hair color.

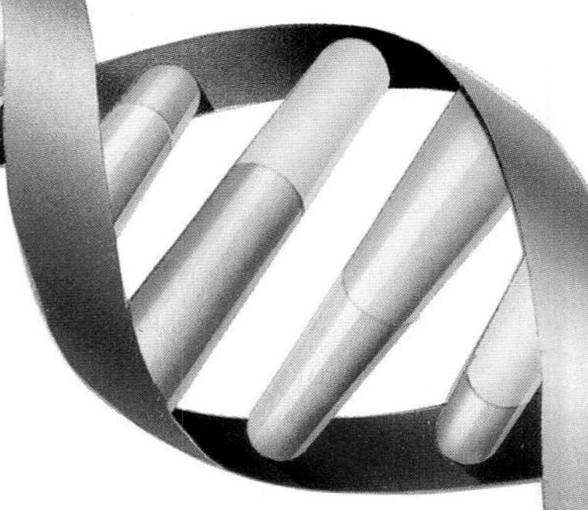

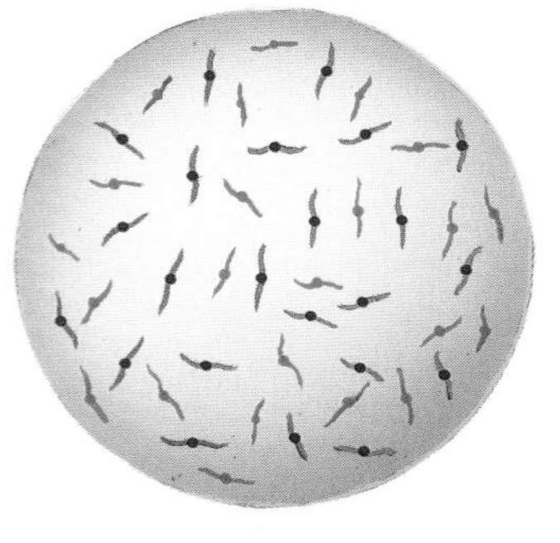

**One of each pair of chromosomes comes from the mother and one from the father.**

**3** Each ovum and each sperm contains 23 chromosomes. When the two join together, the new cell therefore has 46 chromosomes (23 pairs). An exact copy of these 46 chromosomes is passed to every cell in the baby's body and stays with it for life.

## Boy or girl?

Out of the 23 chromosomes in each ovum and each sperm, one is a sex chromosome. There are two types of sex chromosomes. They are called "X" and "Y". All ova have an X chromosome. Half a man's sperm have an X chromosome, the other half have a Y. If a sperm with an X chromosome joins the ovum, the baby will be a girl. If a sperm with a Y chromosome joins the ovum, the baby will be a boy.

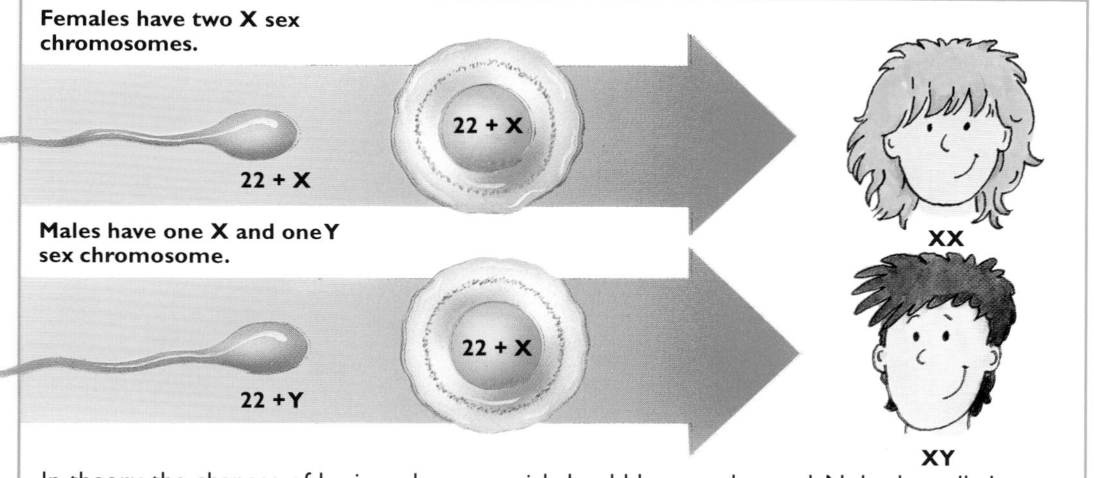


In theory, the chances of having a boy or a girl should be exactly equal. Nobody really knows why some parents seem to produce only boys and others only girls. It is thought that male sperm swim faster but female sperm live longer. Therefore, if a couple have intercourse at the same time as, or after, ovulation, there is more chance of conceiving a boy; if before ovulation, there is more chance of conceiving a girl.

## Which parent will the baby look like?

Many thousands of genes from both parents influence a child's appearance, but instructions about a few characteristics, such as color of hair and eyes, are carried by just one gene from each parent. If the instructions in these two genes conflict, one of them will overrule the other. This one is said to be the "dominant" gene, while the weaker one is said to be "recessive". The genes of the parents shown here could be combined to produce three different hair colors in their children. A dark hair gene overrules other hair colors. A fair hair gene is dominant over a red hair gene. To have red hair, you have to inherit a red hair gene from both your parents.

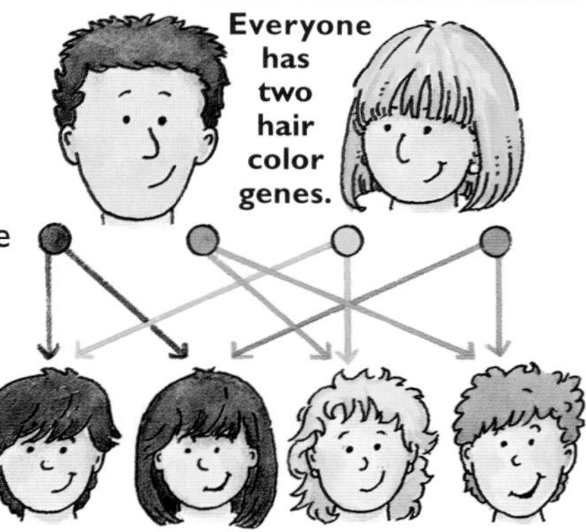

## Abnormal genes

Sometimes a baby acquires an extra chromosome from one or both parents. Down's syndrome babies have three of a certain type of chromosome instead of the usual pair, so the baby has 47 chromosomes altogether instead of 46. This affects the baby's physical and mental development.

Some other disorders which are caused by abnormal genes are passed down from one generation to the next. If there is a family history of a particular disorder, a doctor who specializes in the study of genes can advise a couple on the chances of having a baby affected by it.

# Twins, triplets and test tube babies

The chances of a mother producing twins are about one in 80. In some races they are more common and in some less common than this. A family history of twins, on either the mother's or the father's side, makes twins more likely. Twins, triplets etc. are often referred to as "multiple births".

## How do twins start?

There are two types of twins - identical and nonidentical (fraternal). Identical twins start when a fertilized egg splits in half at a very early stage in its development. Each half develops into a baby.* The twins have identical genes, are the same sex and exactly alike.

Nonidentical twins start when two eggs are released from the mother's ovaries at the same time and are joined by two sperm. These twins may be no more alike than any brother and sister. They may be the same sex or one of each and do not have identical genes.

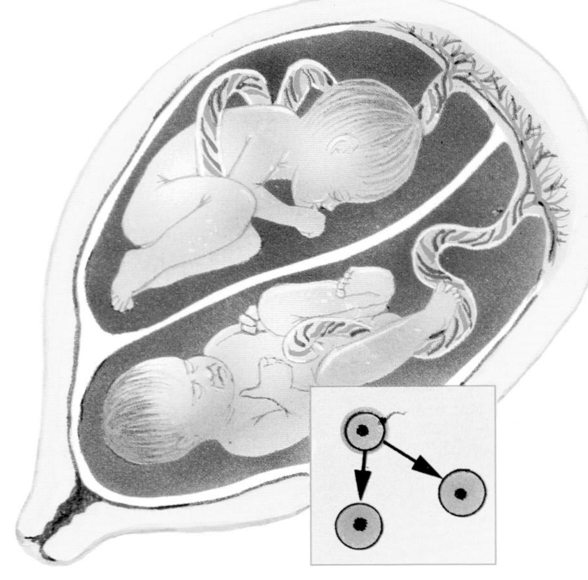

Identical twins share a placenta. The fluid surrounding them is separated by a thin layer of cells enclosed in a common outer layer.

Nonidentical twins each have their own placenta and each is surrounded by its own bag of fluid.

### Diagnosing twins

Sometimes a midwife or doctor may suspect that a woman is going to have twins because her abdomen is much larger than it should be. Sometimes they can detect two heartbeats or feel two heads or lots of limbs. If the mother has an ultrasound scan (see page 64), the twins can usually be detected by the 14th week of pregnancy.

### How twins are born

Labor for a mother giving birth to twins is very similar to labor for a woman having only one baby. It does not usually take longer. There is only one first stage, because once the uterus has opened up, both babies can get out. The second stage is usually very quick for the second baby, because the birth canal has already been stretched by the first.



*If an egg starts to divide but does not completely separate, Siamese twins are produced. This is very rare.*

## Triplets and more

The chance of having triplets is about one in 6,400. Having more than three babies at a time used to be extremely rare. These days, the use of special drugs designed to help women who could not have babies, can sometimes have the effect of stimulating their ovaries to produce more than one egg at a time. Three or more babies can be either identical or nonidentical, or a combination of both.

**Identical (all from one egg)**

**Nonidentical (from three separate eggs)**

**Two identical, one nonidentical**

## Problems in starting a baby

Couples may be unable to have a child or have problems in starting one for a variety of reasons. It may be that the woman is not ovulating, or that the man is not producing healthy sperm, or that the tubes which carry the ova or sperm have become blocked or damaged in some way. Sometimes doctors can give drugs to stimulate ovulation or sperm production. Sometimes they can repair the tubes.

## Test tube babies

*In vitro* fertilization is a method of helping couples who seem unable to start a baby, especially in cases where the cause is blocked uterine tubes. *In vitro* means "in glass" and the method is so-called because test tubes are used in the process. The timing of each step in the process, and the temperature and chemical conditions in which the egg and sperm are kept, have to be extremely carefully controlled for the result to be successful.

The doctor inserts a tube through the woman's abdomen to her ovary, and the ovum she has produced that month is drawn out by suction.

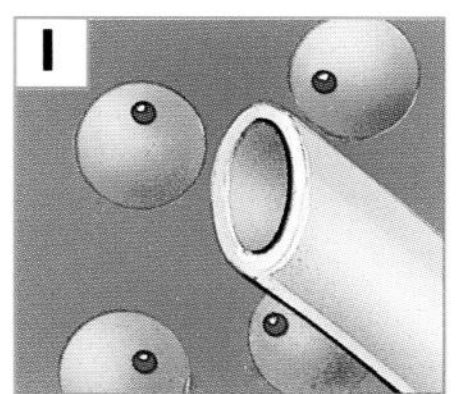


The ovum is put in a dish and the father's sperm is added. One of the sperm fuses with the egg, which then starts to divide and subdivide.

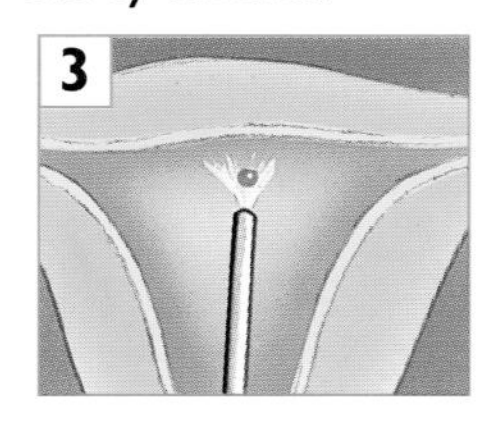


When it has eight or 16 cells, it is put back into the mother's uterus, via a tube inserted through her vagina and cervix.

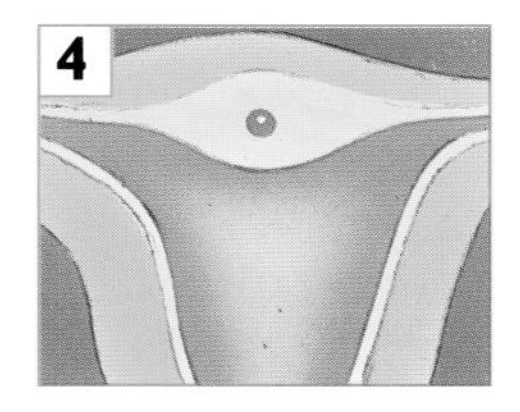


If the fertilized ovum implants itself in the wall of the uterus, it will start to grow there, as in any normal pregnancy.

In cases of *in vitro* fertilization, the woman is often given drugs to encourage her to produce more than one ripened ovum at a time. Several ova are then taken, fertilized and returned to the uterus, to increase the chances of at least one implanting itself. Sometimes they all do.

It is possible to freeze a fertilized ovum for implantation in the uterus at some future date. This means that if one attempt to start a pregnancy is unsuccessful, another can be made without having to operate again to remove ova. Frozen embryos can also be kept in case an attempt is unsuccessful, or a mother wants more children after a successful "test tube" pregnancy.

# Newborn babies

All babies look different and individual, even when they are newly born, but here are a few things you may notice if you see a very new one.

For the first few days, a small piece of the umbilical cord remains attached to the baby's navel. It is tied and sealed with a clip, and soon dries out and falls off.

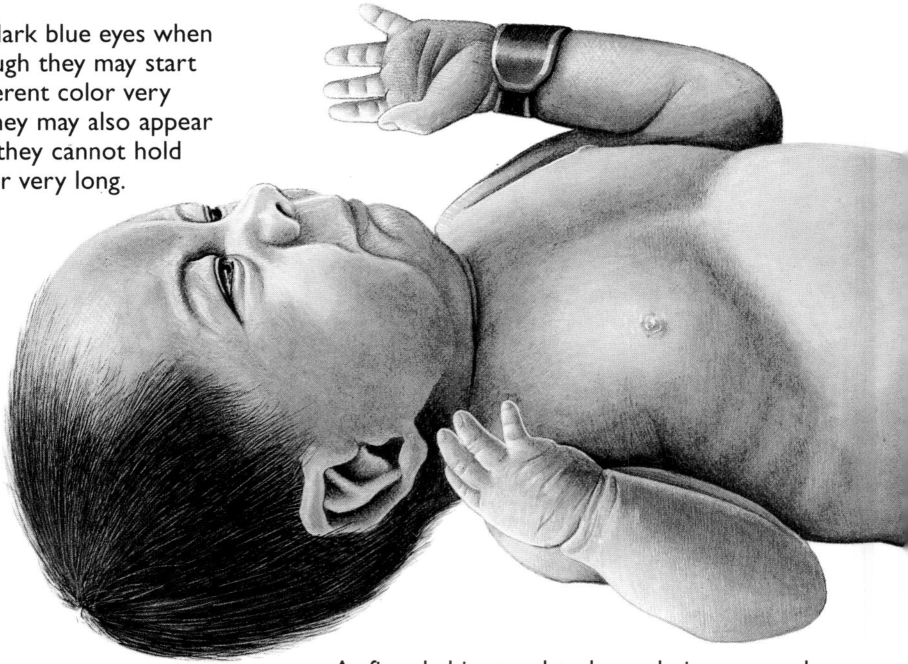

Many babies have dark blue eyes when they are born, though they may start to change to a different color very soon after birth. They may also appear to squint, because they cannot hold both eyes in line for very long.

Some babies are born with quite a mop of hair; others are almost bald. In the womb, babies are completely covered by fine, downy hair. Sometimes they still have some on their bodies and faces, but it soon rubs off.

At first, babies tend to keep their arms and legs close to their bodies, as though they are still enclosed in the womb.

## What is birth like for a baby?

Birth is an experience we have all been through but cannot consciously remember, so we can only imagine what it must be like.

For nine months a baby grows in warmth and comfort in her mother's uterus, surrounded by liquid, darkness and the constant rhythmic sounds of her mother's body. She does not have to breathe or eat; her needs are constantly supplied via her mother's blood.

Suddenly everything changes. The walls of the uterus close in around her, squeezing and pushing her through the narrow passageway to an outside world which is full of completely new sensations. Immediately, her whole body has to adapt to a life more independent of her mother. She has to start breathing and, within a few hours. taking in food, digesting it and expelling her own wastes.

It must come as a great shock to even the most tranquil baby to experience so many new sensations in such a short time. Babies react to this in different ways: some are tired and sleep a great deal at first, others are wide awake; some are upset and jumpy, others serene and contented. Whatever a baby's temperament, most people agree that it is important to introduce a baby to the world as gently as possible, especially during the first few hours after birth. Dim lighting, gentle handling and peaceful surroundings can help to reassure her and make the world a less alarming place.

Many babies develop yellowish skin a few days after birth. This is because it takes a little while before their livers start working properly, so they have slight jaundice. This does not harm them and usually goes away without any treatment.

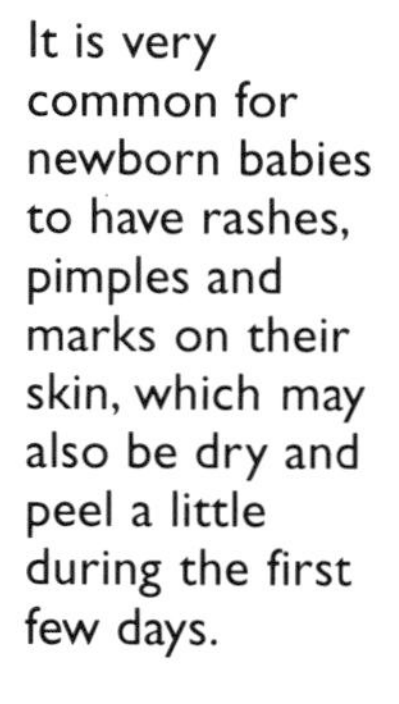

It is very common for newborn babies to have rashes, pimples and marks on their skin, which may also be dry and peel a little during the first few days.

Their finger and toenails are fully formed and sometimes fairly long, but very soft.

On the top of a baby's head, near the front, there is a diamond-shaped patch under the skin, which is not covered by the skull bone. This is called the fontanelle. It usually takes a year or so before the bone completely closes over it. The fontanelle allows the skull bones to overlap a little during the birth, so that the head becomes molded to the shape of the birth canal. This can give it a strange elongated appearance at first. After a few days it becomes rounder.

# New parents

The arrival of a new baby is a very exciting time for the parents and the rest of the family. It is also a time when everyone has to adjust to the presence of a brand new person in their lives. A first child usually brings about great changes in his parents' lives. It takes time to learn how to look after a baby and to get used to being a parent. At first they can feel a little alarmed, overwhelmed and exhausted.

## Getting to know a new baby

It can take varying amounts of time for parents to get to know their new baby and really feel that he belongs to them. Sometimes this happens as soon as he is born, but sometimes he seems like a stranger at first and it takes several days or weeks for a specially close relationship to develop.

It is important that a father has time with his baby and learns to help look after him. The tie between a baby and his mother can be so close that fathers can easily feel left out and jealous.

Brothers and sisters can also feel jealous. However excited they are about the new baby, it can be very hard to see so much attention given to someone new. It helps if they too can spend time with the baby and help to look after him.

## The mother's body

It takes only a few weeks for the main changes in the mother's body to reverse themselves after birth, but it is usually several months before its complete return to normal. The changes start happening the moment the placenta leaves her uterus, since it is the placenta that produces most of the hormones of pregnancy. This sudden change in hormone levels often affects the mother's emotions, making her feel a little tearful and depressed. Occasionally the hormone balance in her body fails to readjust itself and she needs medical treatment for "postnatal" (after birth) depression.

### The uterus

By about six weeks after the birth, the uterus has returned to its normal size. As it shrinks, it contracts and relaxes at irregular intervals. These contractions, known as "after pains", feel similar to period pains and are most obvious in the first few days after the birth.

**Size immediately before the birth.**

**Normal size six weeks after birth: the size of a pear.**

As the uterus shrinks, the extra blood that supplied it is squeezed out, and its thick lining, built up during pregnancy, disintegrates. These pass out of the vagina like a period for up to five or six weeks after the birth.

A new mother needs plenty of rest after her baby is born. The birth itself, the changes taking place in her body and caring for the new baby all use up a great deal of energy.

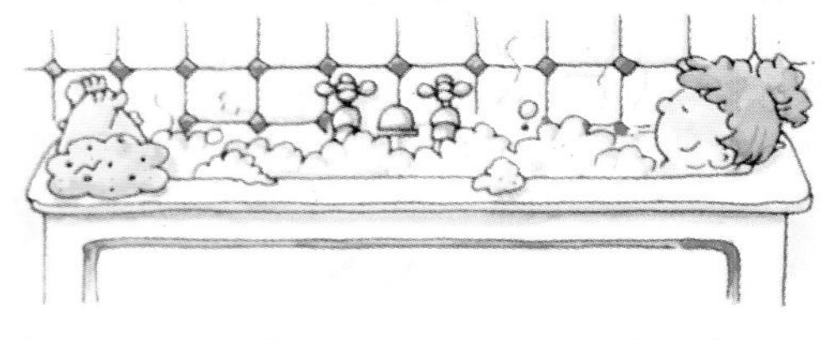

If she has had stitches to repair the skin around her vagina, walking and sitting down will be uncomfortable for a week or so. Hot baths are soothing and help her skin to heal.

Women can usually lose all the extra weight gained during pregnancy but it may take a few months to go. Exercise can help to get rid of it and strengthen muscles that have been stretched. They should also do special exercises designed to strengthen the muscles in the back, abdomen and vagina.

### How soon can another baby start?

A woman does not usually start to ovulate (release eggs) and have periods for at least six weeks after the birth of a baby. From this time onward, she needs to use contraception when having sexual intercourse, unless she wants to start another baby. It may, however, be several months before she starts to ovulate again. Breastfeeding tends to delay but does not prevent it.

# Helping to look after a new baby

When there is a new baby in a family, people usually appreciate all the help they can get, as it is a busy time. The best way of helping may be by doing some shopping, cleaning, washing or cooking. You may also be able to help by looking after the baby. This page gives you an idea of what small babies spend their time doing, but remember that the amount of time spent sleeping, crying or feeding will vary a great deal from one individual to another. The next two pages give some suggestions about how you might help to look after one. Never try to do anything without asking the parents exactly what they want you to do.

Most babies spend between 14 and 18 hours asleep each day, during the first three months of their lives. They sleep in short stretches and wake to feed every few hours throughout the day and night. As they get older, they begin to sleep more at night than during the day.

Crying is a baby's only way of saying that he needs something or that something is wrong, so many babies cry a lot, especially in the first few weeks. Until they are about a month old, crying is more or less the only sound that babies can make, apart from little snuffles and grunts.

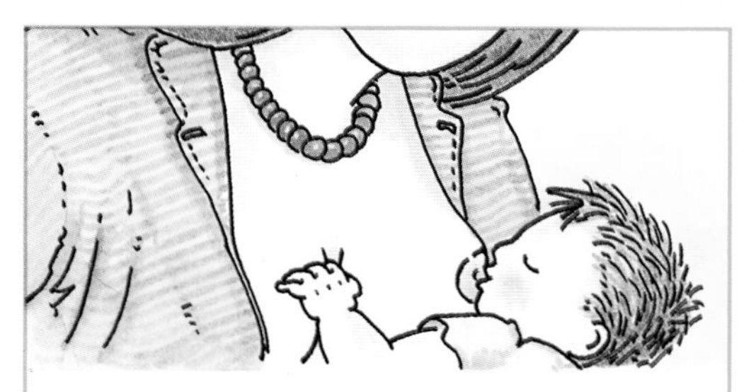

Most young babies need food about every three or four hours, though some may want to feed more often than this. The only food they need is milk, which they get from sucking at a breast or bottle.* They are born knowing instinctively how to suck and swallow.

Newborn babies have very little control over their movements. They have such a strong grip that they can hang from the doctor's fingers. However, this is a reflex (automatic) action and soon disappears. It is a few months before they can grasp things on purpose.

From the moment they are born, babies start using their senses of sight, hearing, smell, touch and taste to learn about the world around them. At first they can only see things clearly if they are about 20cm (8in) from their faces. Everything else is blurred. Over the first few weeks they gradually learn to change the focus of their eyes.

*See pages 82-85.

## What to do if a baby cries

The sound of a baby's crying varies according to what is wrong, but it is often difficult, even for his parents, to figure out what he is trying to say. If a baby cries while you are looking after him and there is no obvious reason, try running through a list of possible causes:

1. He may be hungry - when did he last feed?
2. His diaper may need to be changed (see pages 86-87).
3. Wind may be making him feel uncomfortable or giving him a pain (see page 85).
4. He may be too hot or too cold. (Feel down the back of his neck.)
5. He might be bored or lonely and want some company or entertainment (see below).
6. He may be tired but unable to get to sleep (see opposite page).

## Keeping a baby happy

If a baby does not appear to be hungry, tired or uncomfortable, try some of the things shown below to keep him entertained.

1. Give him things to look at. Babies like looking at bright things, things that move and, above all, people's faces.

2. Give him something to listen to. Babies usually enjoy music and rhythmic noises, and sometimes move their arms and legs in time to the sound. They also like listening to people's voices.

3. Hold him. Babies like the feeling of being held. When you pick a baby up or put him down, keep one hand under his neck and the other under his bottom. Always be careful to keep his head supported because he cannot support it himself. Hold him upright, looking over your shoulder, or lying back with his head supported by the crook of your arm.

4. Rock him. Most babies enjoy the sensation of gentle movement. Try walking up and down while holding him, rocking him in your arms or a cradle, or pushing him in a buggy.

5. Sucking gives babies comfort and pleasure. Some like to suck even when they are not hungry. Some mothers give their babies pacifiers; others help them to find their thumb.

## Helping a baby get to sleep

Some babies fall asleep easily when they are tired, others need help to get to sleep, particularly at certain times of day. Sucking, being rocked or pushed in a buggy and gentle background noise may all help to relax her.

Parents are advised to put their babies to sleep on their sides or backs, not their fronts. Once a baby gets used to a certain position, she may not go to sleep in any other. She cannot turn over by herself at first.

Sometimes the jerks and twitches of her own body as it relaxes into sleep will disturb a baby. She may settle more easily if she is wrapped in a shawl. It should hold her arms firmly to her sides, but her hands should be where she can suck them if she wants to.

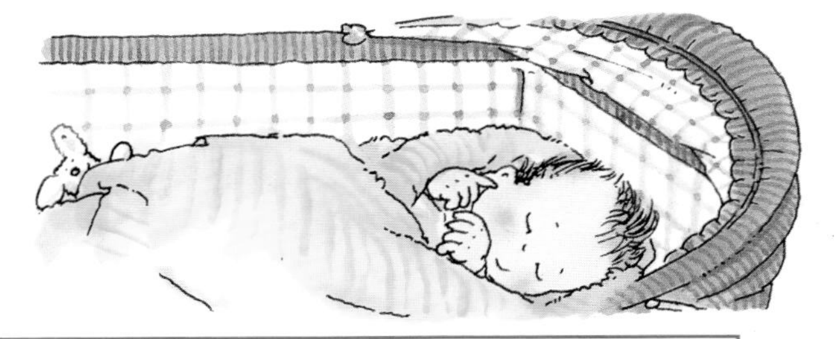

## Getting a bath ready

It is quite difficult to hold a slippery baby safely in a tub full of water, especially if the baby does not enjoy baths. The best way to help with a bath is by getting ready everything that will be needed.

Some mothers bathe their babies every day, but some simply wash their faces, hands and bottoms daily and bathe them every few days. The rest of their bodies do not get very dirty until they start moving around.

An ordinary bathtub is too large and frightening for a tiny baby. Most people use a portable baby bath or bowl for the first few months. A portable bath usually has a stand and you can adjust its height so the bather can sit comfortably on a chair.

1. Use a bowl or pitcher to fill the bath with water. Always put the cold water in first. If you put the hot in first, the plastic of the bath might heat up and scald the baby.

2. Test the water with your elbow - your hands are used to hotter water than the rest of your body. It should feel comfortably warm. Make sure the room is also warm.

3. Collect everything else that will be needed. This includes:
Soap or special baby bath liquid
Cotton balls
Towel
Clean clothes
Diaper changing equipment

# Feeding

For the first few months of their lives the only food that babies need is milk, either from their mothers' breasts or from bottles. After this, they gradually start to have other foods as well as milk and by the time they are about one, they are eating most ordinary foods.

1 Human beings are mammals, which means they produce milk to feed their young. This is the main purpose of women's breasts. Every woman's breasts contain cells for producing milk, but they do not become active unless she has a baby. The changes that prompt the breasts to start producing milk begin during pregnancy and are brought about by the special chemicals called hormones, which are produced by glands* and travel around the body in the blood. The most important hormones involved in the process of breastfeeding are produced by the pituitary gland, which lies at the base of the brain.

## How breastfeeding works

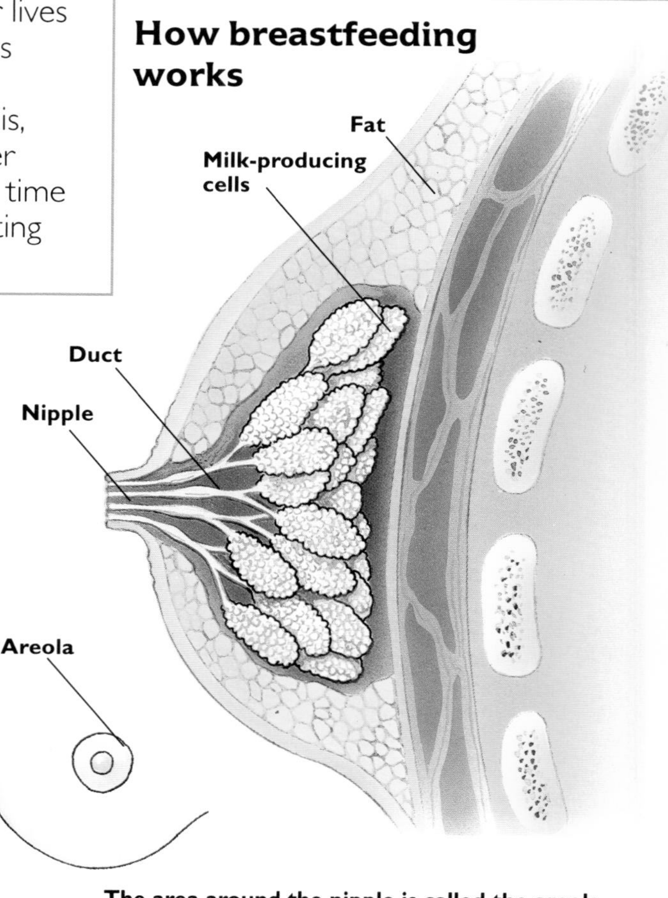


**The area around the nipple is called the areola. The tiny bumps in the areola are glands. During breastfeeding these produce a fluid which helps to protect the nipple and keep it soft and supple.**

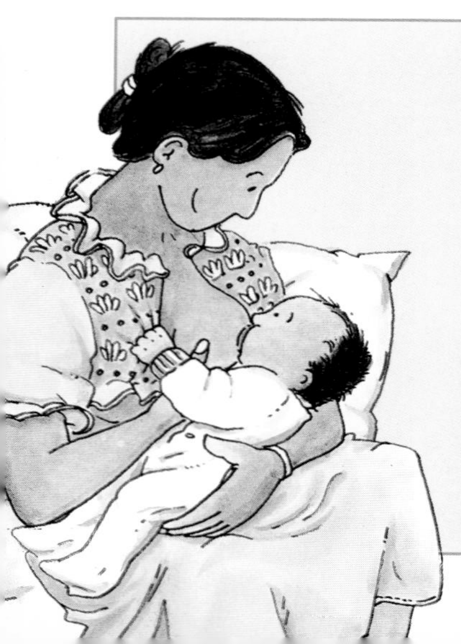

## Some advantages of breastfeeding

Breast milk contains all the ingredients a baby needs in the right proportions and at the right temperature. It is easy for babies to digest and contains germ-fighting proteins called antibodies, which help to protect them from infections. Breast-feeding can give a mother a special feeling of closeness to her baby.

## Why some mothers do not breastfeed

Breastfeeding only works well if the mother is happy to be doing it, and some women dislike it or find it embarrassing. How they feel about it depends a lot on the attitudes of their husbands and their family and friends. Some are put off by initial problems, such as sore nipples. A few have medical problems that prevent them from doing it.

*To find out what a gland is, see page 46.*

Each breast contains milk-producing cells and a network of tubes or ducts, which lead to an opening in the nipple. The milk-producing cells are surrounded by muscle cells and covered by layers of fat, which give each breast its individual shape and size. The fat plays no part in actually making milk, so small breasts are just as good at producing milk as large ones.

During pregnancy the number of ducts and milk-producing cells increases, replacing some of the fat, and the blood supply to the breasts increases. The birth of the baby changes the hormone levels in the blood and these signal to the breasts to start producing milk. The milk is made from substances extracted from the mother's blood as it passes through her breasts. Once made, it drains into the ducts.

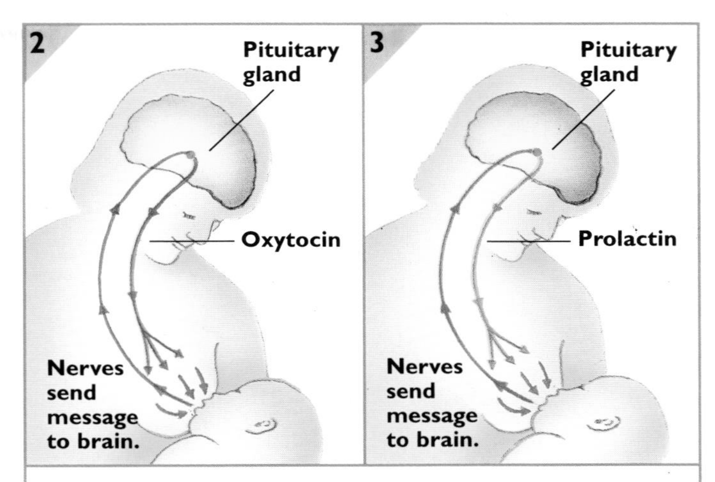


A baby sucking at its mother's breast stimulates sensitive nerve-endings in the nipple, which send messages to the brain. The brain instructs the pituitary gland to produce a hormone called oxytocin. Oxytocin makes the muscle cells around the milk-producing cells and ducts contract and this forces milk down the ducts and out of the nipples. This process is known as the "let-down reflex". It only works if the mother is feeling relaxed and calm.

The baby's sucking also stimulates the pituitary gland to produce another important hormone, called prolactin. This is the hormone which tells the breasts to produce more milk. The amount of sucking the baby does therefore directly controls the amount of milk that is produced. When a mother wants to stop breastfeeding, she slowly cuts down the baby's sucking time and the amount of milk is gradually reduced.

## Things a breastfeeding mother needs to do

In order to produce enough milk for the baby and satisfy the needs of her own body, a breastfeeding mother needs to eat plenty of nourishing food: breastfeeding uses between 600 and 800 extra calories a day. She also needs to drink plenty of liquid and to rest as much as possible.

The things a mother eats and drinks affect the content and taste of her milk. There is no food she definitely has to avoid, but certain foods may upset certain babies. Alcohol can pass into the milk but probably does no harm in small amounts. Nicotine, certain medicines and other drugs can also pass into the milk.

## Bottle feeding

For mothers who decide to bottle feed their babies, preparing formula and cleaning bottles and equipment can take up quite a lot of time. You might be able to help by doing this, or by actually giving the baby a bottle. You would have to get the baby's mother or father to show you exactly what to do, but you may find some useful tips and reminders here.

## Fighting germs

A new baby's body has had no time to build up resistance to the germs which are all around us and generally do no harm to older people. Milk, especially warm milk, is an ideal breeding ground for germs. It is very important that everything that goes in young babies' mouths or touches their milk is sterile (free from germs). There are two methods of sterilizing feeding equipment. Whichever is used, the equipment must be absolutely clean before sterilizing begins.

1. You put the bottles, nipples etc. in a steam sterilizer with a little water and switch on. The steam that is created sterilizes the equipment in about 10 minutes.

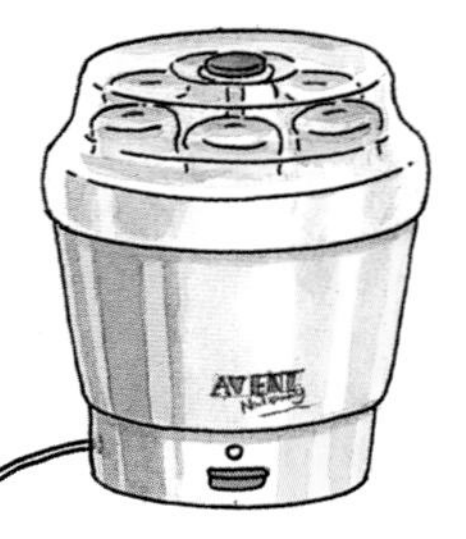

2. You soak the equipment in a chemical sterilizing solution. The chemicals come in the form of tablets, crystals or liquids to which you add water. To mix up the solution you follow the instructions on the packet. You usually have to soak things for at least half an hour before they are sterilized.

Here are some other important rules to help fight germs:
*Always wash your hands before handling a bottle or mixing up formula.
*All water given to a baby in any form must first be boiled to make it sterile, then cooled.
* Once mixed, formula must be used immediately or stored in a refrigerator. Milk at room temperature breeds germs.

## Milk and bottles

You cannot give babies ordinary cow's milk until they are about a year old, because it is too difficult for them to digest. There are many different brands of specially prepared milk for bottle-fed babies. Most are based on cow's milk which has been modified by various processes to make it as like human milk as possible. This is often referred to as "formula" milk and usually comes in powdered form.

## Feeding

First, test the temperature of the milk by letting a few drops fall on the inside of your wrist. The milk should come at several drops a second and feel just warm. Babies prefer it at this temperature, though cold milk is not bad for them. If it is too cold, stand the bottle in a bowl of warm water; if it is too hot, stand it in the refrigerator.

Make yourself comfortable in a chair, with the baby cradled in one arm. The baby should be fairly upright, with her head well above her stomach. Support your arm with cushions, otherwise it will ache.

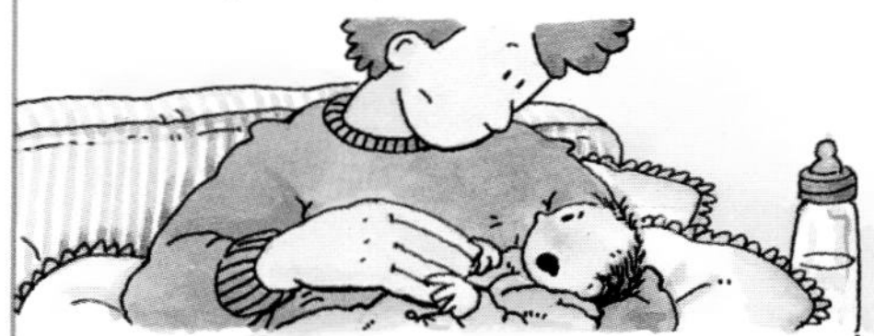

You could put a cloth around the baby's neck or have one handy, ready to mop up dribbles.

Formula milk has to be mixed with boiled water. Instructions about how to do this are given on each container. It is very important to follow them carefully and use exactly the right amount of powder. It is very bad for a baby to have too rich a mixture.

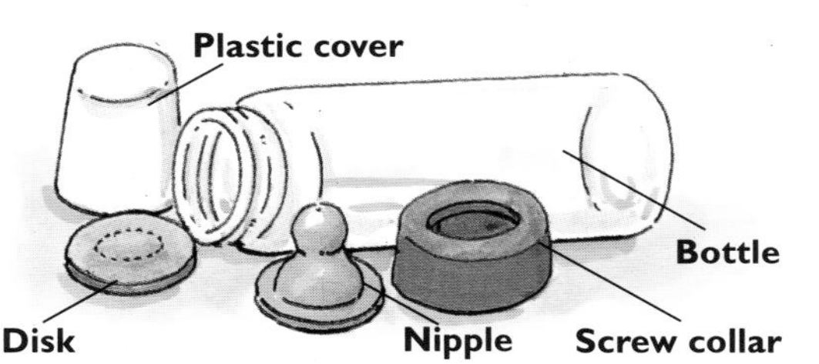


Most feeding bottles are made of glass or plastic and have a rubber nipple which fits onto the bottle with a screw collar. There is also a plastic cover for the nipple and a disk to use under the collar, if you want to seal the bottle so that milk cannot leak out.

Touch the baby on the cheek that is nearer to you. She will turn her head toward you.

Touch her lips with the nipple and she will take it into her mouth and start sucking. Make sure the nipple goes well back in her mouth and keep the bottle tipped up so the nipple is always full of milk, not air.

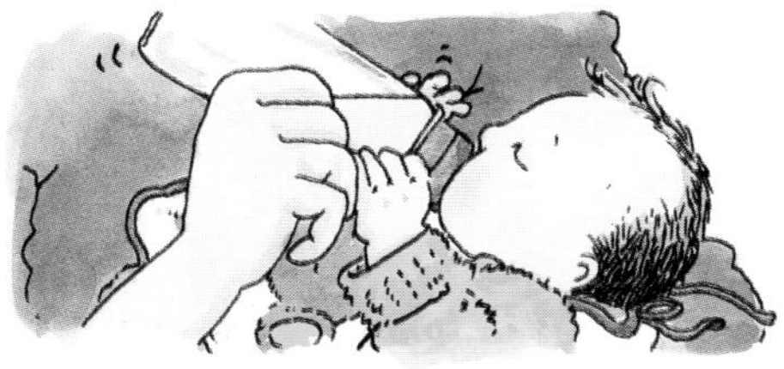

During feeding the nipple may flatten and stop milk from getting out. If this happens, pull it gently away from the side of the baby's mouth, so a little air can get into the bottle.

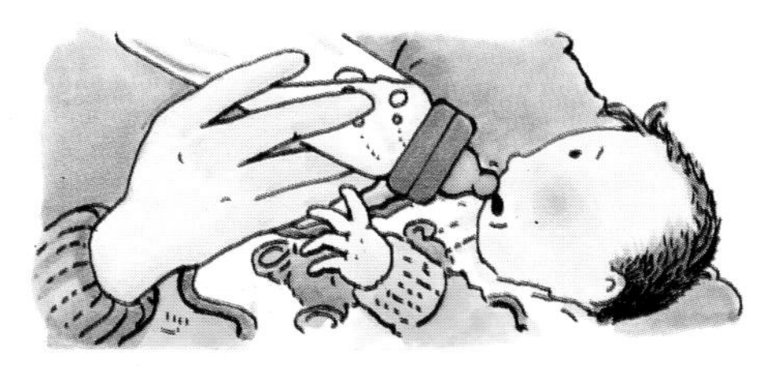

The baby may need breaks during feeding. She will stop sucking and let go of the bottle. She may also need to be burped (see right). If you have burped her and she still does not want the bottle, she has probably had enough.

## Burping

Most babies tend to swallow some air while they are feeding. This goes down to their stomachs with their milk and can make them feel uncomfortably full or give them pain. If this happens, they need to burp air up.

Milk is heavier than air. If you keep the baby in a fairly upright position, the air will rise above the milk and escape more easily.

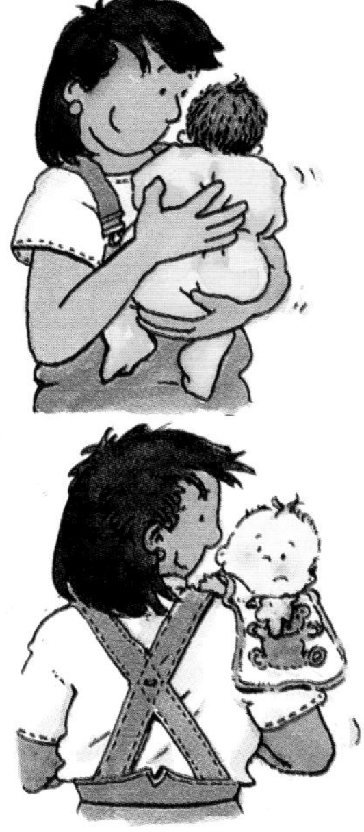

To get air up, all you need to do is hold the baby upright. If she does not burp after a minute or two, gently rub or pat her back. If she still does not burp, she may not have any air.

## Bringing up milk

If there is air below the milk in the baby's stomach, she may bring up a little milk when she burps. She may also bring up milk if she has swallowed more than she could comfortably hold. Babies often do this. It is nothing to worry about.

## Hiccups

Babies often get hiccups, especially after feeding. It does not seem to bother them and does no harm.

# Diapers

Changing a diaper is a very useful way of helping to look after a baby. A newborn baby needs to be changed about six to eight times a day and most babies continue to wear diapers until they are at least two years old. It is usual to change a diaper before or after each feeding and whenever else you suspect it is dirty. Everyone tends to develop their own particular diaper-changing routine, so you will need to watch what a baby's parents normally do before attempting a change yourself. The information given here will then remind you what to do.

## Different types of diapers

There are two main types of diapers: cloth, which you wash after each use, and disposable, which you throw away.

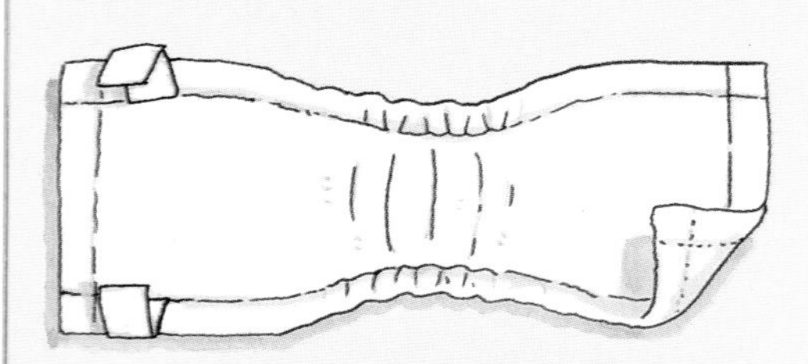

Disposable diapers consist of absorbent padding backed by plastic. They usually have adhesive tabs with which to fasten them. There are many different brands of disposables and there are different shapes to fit girls and boys.

Washable diapers consist of either a triangle or square of cloth. Square diapers need to be folded before you use them. You fasten them with diaper pins (large safety pins with special safety hoods to stop them from snapping open).

## Changing a diaper

**1** Before you start, check that you have everything you need within reach, so that you do not have to leave the baby while you find things. You will need:

1 A plastic covered *changing mat* or a *towel* on which to lay the baby.
2 Special *baby wipes*, or *cotton balls* and *baby lotion* or a small bowl of *warm water*, for cleaning the baby's bottom.
3 *Cream* to protect the baby's bottom.
4 A *clean diaper* plus a *liner* and *plastic pants*, if used. Make sure you fold a cloth diaper before you start and that you have diaper pins.
5 A *pail* or *plastic bag* for the dirty diaper.
6 A *clean set of clothes* in case the diaper has leaked.

**2** You can lay the baby across your knees, but it is probably easier to lay him on a changing mat or folded towel on a flat surface in front of you. The floor is the safest place.

**3** Undo the baby's diaper and lift his bottom in the air by holding both ankles in one hand with a finger between them. With the other hand, remove the dirty diaper.

## Diaper liners

Diaper liners are squares of disposable material designed to be placed inside cloth diapers to stop them from getting so dirty. There are also washable "one-way" diaper liners, which keep the baby's bottom drier by letting urine through one way but not back the other.

## Plastic pants

Plastic pants are an extra that can be used with any type of diaper. Some have elasticated legs and waists and simply pull on. Others fasten with snaps at the sides. Some are made of very soft plastic which you tie in a knot at both sides, or at the front and back.

## Three ways to fold a diaper

Different ways of folding diapers suit babies of different ages, shapes, sizes and sex. Here are three for you to try.

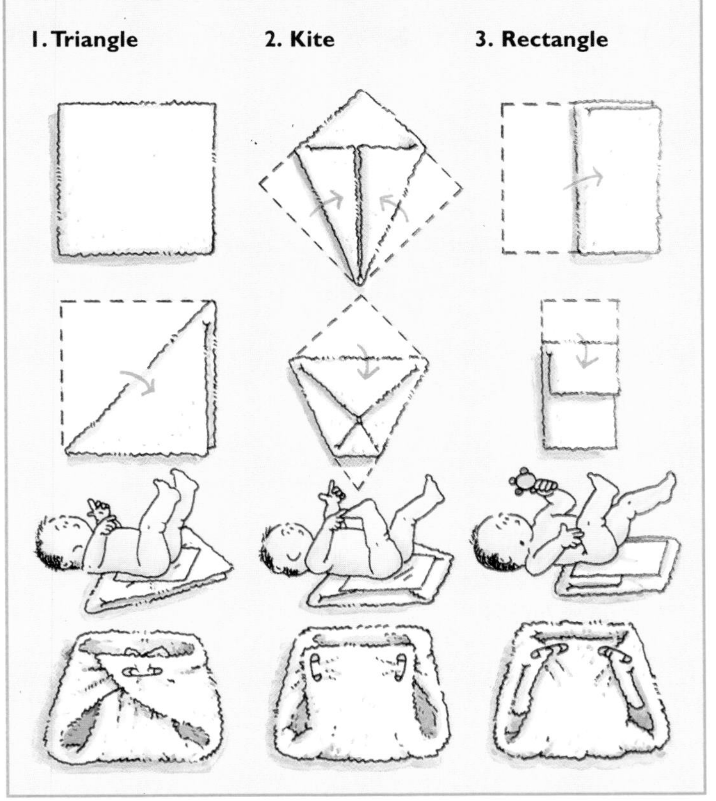

Clean the baby's bottom thoroughly using baby wipes, or cotton balls and baby lotion or warm water. If you use water, make sure you dry the skin carefully afterward.

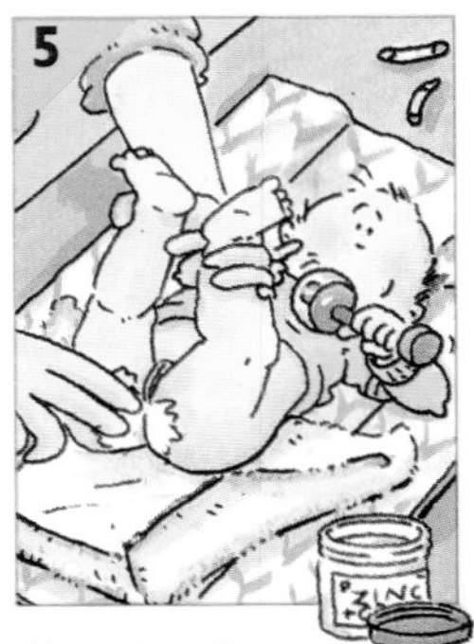


Put the clean diaper in position under the baby and then put some protective cream on his bottom. This helps to prevent moisture reaching his skin and giving him "diaper rash".

**6** Bring the front part of the diaper up through the baby's legs and fasten it. With a disposable, be careful not to get cream on the sticky tabs as this will stop them from sticking and you may have to add adhesive tape. With a cloth diaper, keep some of your fingers between the baby's skin and the diaper pin, when you fasten it, to make sure you do not prick the baby.

**7** Wash your hands.

# Growing and learning

Babies start life with very little control over their bodies, but during the first year or so they rapidly learn to move the different parts of their bodies at their own will. Their control develops from the head downward, ending with the legs and feet.

Different babies develop at very different rates and early development seems to bear little relation to ability later in life. The ages given in this section give only an indication of when each development may happen; there can be very wide variations. All babies, however, tend to go through the same stages and in the same order. If you know a baby, see if you can tell which stage she has reached in each of the sections below.

## Learning to support head

**At birth**
**When a baby is lifted up, his head flops because his neck muscles cannot support it. When lying on his front, he can lift his head just enough to turn his face to one side.**

**At 6 weeks**
**He can turn his head from side to side, when lying on his back. On his front, he can lift his head up for a few seconds.**

**At 3 months**
**He can lift his head and shoulders when lying on his front and hold his head steady when held upright.**

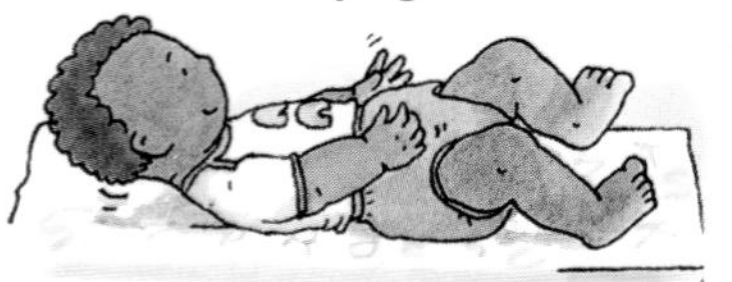

**At 6 months**
**He can lift his head when lying on his back.**

## Learning to use hands

**At 3 months**
**A baby has "discovered" her hands. She plays with them and watches them, can briefly hold things placed in them, and starts reaching out to touch things.**

**At 6 months**
**She pats and strokes things, can reach out and grasp things in both hands and transfer things from one hand to the other.**

**At 7 months**
**She can pick things up with only one hand, holding her fingers and thumb together like a scoop. She may offer them to other people, but does not know how to let go of them.**

**At 9 months**
**She starts to gain control over each finger separately and points to things, using just one finger.**

**At 11 months**
**She learns to grip things between her fingers and thumb and can now pick up very small objects.**

**At 12 months**
**She learns to let go of things by deliberately uncurling her fingers.**

## Rolling over

**At birth**
**A new baby's natural position is all curled up.**

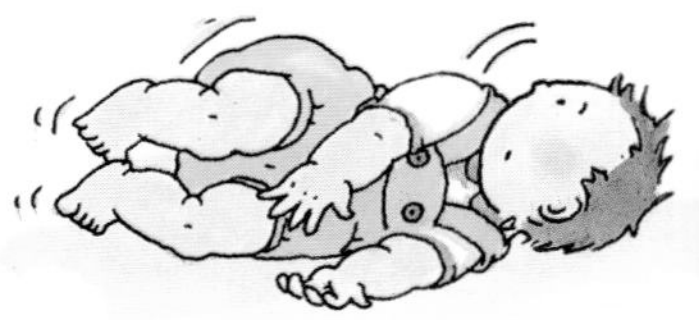

**At 3 months**
**His body has straightened out. He learns to roll from his back to his side and back again.**

**At 4 months**
**He learns to roll from his front onto his back.**

**At 6 months**
**He learns to roll from his back to his front.**

**At 8 months**
**Some babies learn to move around by rolling over and over.**

## Learning to sit

**At birth**
If you try to place a baby in a sitting position, her back curves forward and her head flops onto her knees.

**At 6 weeks**
She can be propped up in a sitting position by using cushions or a baby chair.

**At 4 months**
If you support her arms, she can hold a sitting position.

**At 6 months**
She can sit unsupported for a few seconds but her balance is bad. The bottom of her back is still curved.

**At 7 months**
She may put her hands on the floor to help her balance.

**At 8 months**
She can sit unsupported if she keeps still.

**At 9 months**
She can reach forward for toys and learns to twist around to reach things to the side or behind her. She may later start to move by shuffling along on her bottom.

**At 12 months**
She learns to lie down again by rolling over to one side and breaking her fall.

## Learning to crawl

**At 4 months**
He can lift his head and shoulders by taking the weight on his arms and hands.

**At 5 months**
He raises both his chest and legs off the floor and makes swimming movements.

**At 6 months**
He bends his knees up under his body and gets into a crawling position.

**At 8 months**
He rocks backward and forward and swivels around but cannot move along.

**At 9 months**
He learns to coordinate his arm and leg movements to move himself along. Babies often move backward before they can move forward, because their arms are stronger and better coordinated than their legs.

## Standing and walking

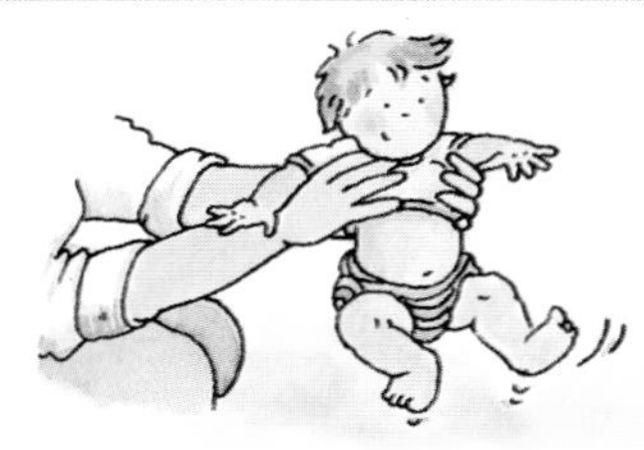

**At 6 months**
She bounces up and down, by bending and straightening her legs when held upright with her feet touching a firm surface. She then starts to bounce from one foot to the other and later puts one foot in front of the other.

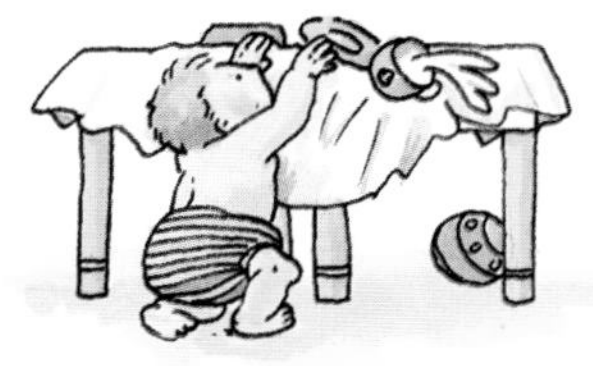

**At 10 months**
She can take her own weight on her feet by now but cannot balance. She uses furniture or people to pull herself from a sitting or kneeling to a standing position. At first she cannot sit down again without help.

**At 11 months**
She walks forward if her hands are held.

**At 12 months**
She walks sideways, holding onto furniture.

**At 13 months**
She stands unsupported and learns to walk a step between gaps in the furniture.

**At 15 months**
She walks fairly steadily for short distances.

## Growing and changing shape

Although babies of the same age vary enormously in size and weight, the first two years of life are a time of very rapid growth for all babies. The speed and amount of growth depends largely on characteristics inherited from both parents.

During the first week of life, most babies lose weight, regaining their birth weight by the time they are 10 days old. A baby of average size weighs roughly twice his birth weight at six months old and three times his birth weight at the end of his first year.

A baby's height increases by approximately half during the first year. By the time a girl is 18 months old, she has reached roughly half her adult height. Boys reach half their adult height at about two years old.

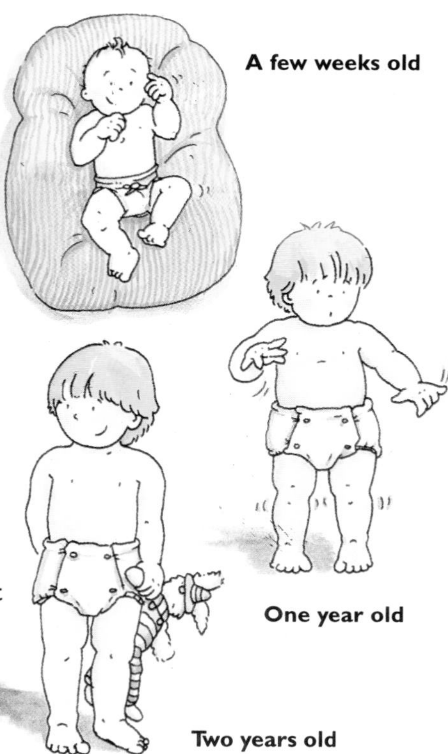


The proportions of the body change throughout childhood and adolescence, but the changes are especially noticeable during the first two years. During the first year, the head becomes a smaller proportion of the whole body, although it does increase in size very rapidly. The legs and arms get longer in proportion to the rest of the body. During the second year, the body elongates and looks firmer and more muscular.

## Teeth

Most babies are born without any teeth showing through their gums. The first one often appears after about six months, but it is not unusual to wait a year before any teeth come through. Occasionally, a baby may be born with a tooth already visible. By the time they are three, most children have a full set. Sometimes, as a tooth pushes its way through the gum, it can be painful for the baby. This may make him miserable and irritable. It may also make him dribble and give him red, blotchy patches on his cheeks.

There are 20 teeth in the first, or "milk" set. (The second set consists of 32 teeth. It does not start appearing until a child is about six or seven.)

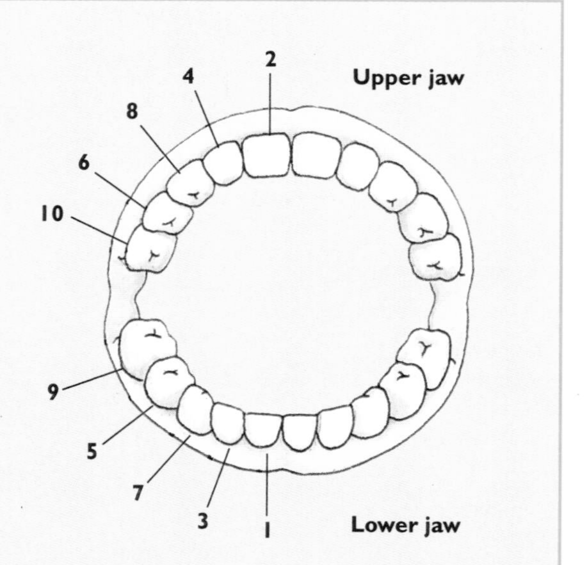


The teeth usually appear in the order shown here. Only half the set is numbered, because matching pairs from both sides of the mouth tend to appear at about the same time.

## Playing and learning

Babies learn very rapidly during their first two years, and playing is one of their main ways of learning and trying out what they have learned. When you play with them, give them plenty of time to take things in and react to them - they have much slower reactions than older children. Most babies have a short attention span, though they may enjoy some games so much that they want to play them over and over again. They need plenty of variety in the things they play with, but games with people and all sorts of ordinary household objects can entertain and teach them just as much as bought toys. Below are some play ideas, divided into four age categories.

## Learning to talk

A baby starts to communicate with the people around her long before she can talk. She does this by her expressions and movements, by smiling (from about six weeks) and laughing (from about four months) and by using a great variety of sounds. The more you respond to her, the more she will want to communicate. Gradually, she starts to recognize certain sounds, realize they have a meaning and try to make them herself. She will probably understand a great many words before she can say anything at all herself. Below is a rough outline of the stages in learning to talk.

**0 to 6 weeks**
**Cries.**
**Silently opens and closes mouth.**

**At 6 weeks**
**Gurgles**

**At 4 months**
**Makes cooing noises - at first long vowel sounds, later adds first consonants.**

**At 7 months**
**Starts making two-syllabled "babbling" sounds by repeating the first syllable.**

**At 8 months**
**Makes more and more complicated sounds. Shouts to attract attention.**

ah-dee-bah-moo-cah

**At 9 months**
**Joins up a variety of different sounds into "sentences". Tries out different intonation patterns.**

**At 12 months**
**Uses first real words. These are nearly always labels for people or things. May make up own words. Over the next few months, slowly learns more words.**

**At 18 months**
**Starts learning new words more rapidly.**

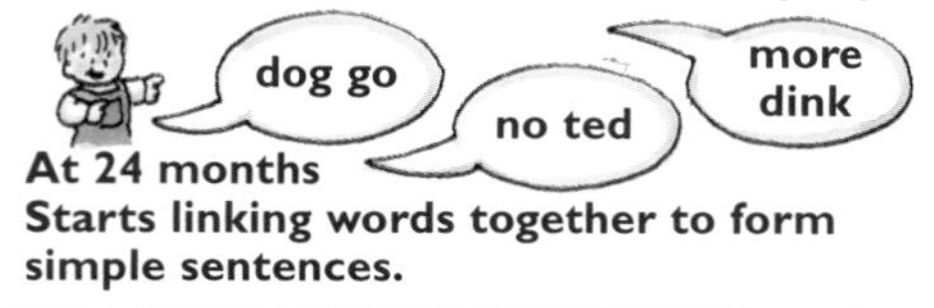


**At 24 months**
**Starts linking words together to form simple sentences.**

## Becoming more independent

As babies gain more control over their own bodies and more understanding of the world around them, they start to become less dependent on other people and do more things for themselves. Below are two of the biggest steps toward independence that a small child makes.

**1** Sometime between three and six months old, a baby starts to need more than just milk to satisfy his hunger. He can then have small tastes of a variety of everyday foods that have been mushed to a purée. The amounts are gradually increased until he is having solid food (not just milk) at every meal.

Soon he learns to chew food and can pick up things in his fingers and get them into his mouth. Then he starts to grab hold of the spoon and, a little later, manages to use it to put some food in his mouth. With constant practice he gets better and better at using the spoon, until he can feed himself a complete meal.

Sometime during the second year, a baby starts to be aware in advance when he is about to dirty or wet his diaper. Once he can give warning of this, he can be taught to sit on a potty instead. It can take him several months to learn to use the potty every time he needs it. When he knows how to use a potty, he can learn to use the toilet. He will need holding steady on the seat and help with undressing and dressing for some time.

# Babysitter's guide

On this page and the next one are some questions to ask and safety tips to remember when you look after a baby or young child on your own. To make it easier for you, the information is divided into two sections: the first is about looking after babies who are not yet moving around by themselves; the second about looking after older babies and toddlers.

When you babysit, it is very important to think of everything you might want to know, and find out exactly what you are expected to do, before the parents leave.

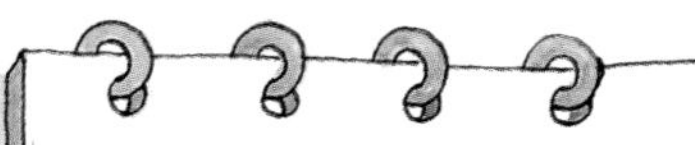

## Telephone numbers

Always make sure you have:

1 The telephone number and address of the place where the parents are going.
2 The telephone number of the child's doctor.
3 The telephone number of an adult friend or relative who lives nearby.

## Questions to ask (young babies)

Will she need to be given a bottle? If yes, should you give her juice, boiled water, or milk? Should it be warm or cold? What time should you give it? Get exact instructions about how to prepare milk.

Will she need a diaper change? Where are the diapers and changing equipment? What is the normal diaper-changing routine?

Is she likely to want to sleep? Does she have any comfort habits to help her get to sleep? Does she sleep on her back or her side?

## Safety tips (young babies)

**Never leave a baby alone with a bottle - she might choke.**

**Never give a baby a pillow to sleep on.**

**Don't put bouncy baby chairs on tables or sofas. They can sometimes move as they bounce and fall off.**

**Make sure that strong sunlight is not shining into the baby's face.**

**Don't leave a baby lying on a bed or table. Even if she cannot crawl, she may wiggle or roll off.**

**Hold the bannisters while you carry a baby up or down stairs. It is easy to trip and lose your balance.**

**Don't let toddlers pick the baby up.**

**If there is a cat in the house, make sure it does not get into the baby's crib. Cats like snuggling up in warm places, but might lie on top of the baby and smother her.**

**Be very careful to keep hot drinks away from a baby. A spill could be dangerous.**

**Watch that the baby does not put anything in her mouth.**

## Questions to ask (older babies)

When babies become more aware of what is going on around them, they usually need a little time to get to know a new babysitter before their parents leave. They also like to have everything done in exactly the way they are used to.

Do you need to give him any food or drink? Which cup, plate and spoon should you use? Does he need a bib? Which chair does he use?

Will you need to change a diaper, or help him to use the potty or toilet? What does he call the toilet?

What time does he go to bed? What is his normal bedtime routine? Does he have a comfort object, or a favorite toy or book to take to bed? What should you do if he will not go to sleep, or wakes up crying?

## Safety tips (older babies)

**Do not leave a mobile baby alone in a room, unless he is in a cot.**

**When he climbs onto things, be ready to catch him if he falls off.**

**Beware that he does not put sharp things, or things that could choke him, into his mouth.**

**Watch him carefully on steps and stairs.**

**Do not let him play with plastic bags.**

**Watch out for things he might try to pull, such as the cord of an iron, a pot handle on a stove, or a tablecloth hanging within reach.**

**Keep knives, scissors, pins, needles, matches, glasses and mugs of hot drinks well out of reach.**

**Keep him away from electric sockets and plugs, and hot ovens and radiators.**

**Toddlers may want to taste medicines and household cleaners. Make sure they do not get hold of any.**

**Never leave a baby or toddler alone in a high chair.**

**Never leave a baby or toddler alone in a bathtub, or playing with water in a bowl or sink.**

**Playing with doors can easily lead to trapped fingers and banged heads.**

# Index